COVER
Detail from *Reconnaissance Geologic Map of the Madras Quadrangle* (1968) by A. C. Waters.

ISSUE 4 / FALL 2024
A FAITH MATTERS PUBLICATION

wayfaremagazine.org

*ISSUE 4 (FALL 2024)*
WAYFARE MAGAZINE IS PUBLISHED BY THE FAITH MATTERS FOUNDATION
FOR INQUIRIES, PLEASE CONTACT WAYFARE@FAITHMATTERS.ORG

*Maurice Denis*

# ESSAYS

# POEMS

# STORY

# COMIC

# EXHIBITS

# INTERVIEW

# HYMN

# BECOMING SAINTS

ZACHARY
DAVIS

*"The only real sadness, the only real failure,
the only great tragedy in life,
is not to become a saint."*
-Léon Bloy

W HO WAS THE FIRST CHRIS-
tian saint? That depends on how
one defines the term. If *saint* means
remarkably devoted follower of Jesus, the first
is probably his mother Mary, who accepted with
faith Gabriel's message. If *saint* means special
proclaimer of the good news of Christ, then John
the Baptist, or perhaps Simon Peter, who were
the first to recognize Jesus as the messiah. If
*saint* is defined the way Catholics use the word,
as someone residing in heaven, then the first is
technically Dismas, the penitent thief who Jesus
promised on the cross would be with him that
day in paradise. Or, by that logic, perhaps those
raised to heaven even earlier, such as Moses,
Elijah, or Enoch. On the other hand, if a saint
is someone who dies testifying of Christ, then,
as the first martyr, Stephen has the best claim,
having been stoned to death by the Sanhedrin
for his witness.

These are generally the kinds of people we
have in mind when we think of the word *saint*—
individuals exemplifying heroic faith, virtue,
character, and sacrifice. People worthy of emula-
tion and veneration.

But *saint* didn't originally have this meaning.
The English word is derived from the Latin
*sanctus*, which represents the Greek *hagios*
and the Hebrew *qādōsh*. These words, *sanctus*,
*hagios*, *qādōsh*, were applied to God, but also to
people and things consecrated and set apart for
a sacred purpose or office—made "holy to God."
Jerusalem was the holy city not because its resi-
dents were especially righteous (usually quite the
contrary), but because it had been chosen by God
and set apart for a special purpose. *Sanctus*, when
applied to a person, did not necessarily connote
high moral quality.

*Above: Early & Latter-day Saints by Charlotte Alba*

In fact, initially, the word *saint* did not refer
to individuals at all, but to a community. For
instance, in his letters, Paul addresses himself
to the saints in Achaia, at Ephesus, at Philippi, at
Colossae. By *saints* he means all the members of
the Christian communities in those places, God's
holy people, the New Israel. It did not mean that
all Christians had achieved a state of perfect
moral rectitude, but that they also had been called
to God's service and were now together learning
how to "turn away from evil and do good," to
"strive for peace," and to live "as becometh saints."

In time, the term *saint* came to be applied to
particular categories among the faithful: to those
who had died "in the Lord," to the martyrs, and
to the first monks. At the same time, *saint* in the
singular began to be used as a term of individual
appreciation or as a sort of official title, especially
for a bishop. Only later did *saint* became the title
of honor and respect used individually for persons

distinguished among their fellow Christians for the degree of their devotion to Christ.

Early Christians soon began to call on those who had received this honorific in prayer, entreating these holy inhabitants of heaven to intercede on their behalf. They revered and treasured the bodily remains of the saints and named their children and churches after them. And each year on the anniversary of the saint's death, the faithful would gather at the grave, celebrate the Eucharist, and have a "feast day"—an occasion not of mourning but of rejoicing and triumph, and the root of our word *festival*.

The first such annual commemoration of which there is record is that of Polycarp, Bishop of Smyrna (modern day Turkey). He was probably the last person to have known an apostle, having been a disciple of St. John. At age eighty-six, Polycarp was captured and led into the crowded Smyrna stadium to be burned alive. He miraculously survived the flames, requiring his Roman persecutors to finish off the job by stabbing him with a dagger.

St. Polycarp wasn't the only early martyr who had to be killed twice. St. Sebastian, sentenced to death by the emperor Diocletian for converting fellow prisoners (and even the warden), was tied to a tree and riddled with arrows. Revived with divine help, Sebastian marched back to the emperor to call him to repentance and was finally beaten to death with clubs. Even more dramatically, after being decapitated, St. Denis, a third-century bishop of Paris, calmly picked up his head, walked six miles, gave a sermon, and finally collapsed.

Over the centuries, accounts of saints proliferated, and Roman Catholics today recognize more than ten thousand. There are patron saints for every country, profession, and circumstance you can think of. Lost your keys? A prayer to St. Anthony of Padua might help. Love animals and the natural world? St. Francis of Assisi is your man. Seeking ecstatic union with God? St. Teresa of Ávila shows the way.

Some saints were beloved for their sense of humor. St. Lawrence, one of the early deacons

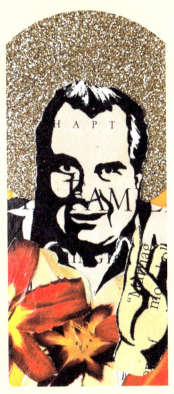

of Rome, was being roasted on a gridiron when he allegedly told his torturers, "Turn me over; I'm done on this side." Some saints could fly. St. Joseph of Cupertino, a "remarkably unclever" seventeenth-century priest, would levitate every time he heard the name of Jesus during mass, often to the consternation of his superiors. St. Christopher was seven feet tall with a dog head, while St. Guinefort was an actual dog—a thirteenth-century French greyhound revered for saving an infant from a snake.

For the first thousand years of Christian life, local bishops were charged with recognizing new saints. But as the Church grew, some of the more outlandish local saint veneration began to be embarrassing in the eyes of higher-up clergy. The need for a more standardized process became apparent, involving detailed investigations into the life and miracles of the candidate and ultimate approval by the pope. In 993, this new system for sainthood was implemented when Pope John xv formally canonized St. Ulrich of Augsburg, known for aiding women in pregnancy.

In a further refinement, the Office of the Devil's Advocate was established in 1587, in a strategy to sift out all but the truly genuine miracles qualifying candidates for sainthood.

For the Protestant reformers, though, a rigorous review process didn't address their more fundamental problems with saints. Luther rejected the idea that certain individuals had a higher spiritual status or special access to God. In a return to the New Testament concept, he taught that all people became saints through their faith in Christ—a "priesthood of all believers"—and there was no need for a special class of Christians. The veneration of saints and the practice of asking for their intercession were both condemned as unbiblical.

When Joseph Smith organized his church on April 6, 1830, it was called The Church of Christ. Four years later, the name was changed to "The Church of the Latter Day Saints," probably to avoid being confused for Alexander Campbell's movement, also called The Church of Christ. Oliver Cowdery wrote in editorials at the time that it was "reasonable" that God "should call his people by a name which would distinguish them from all other people." The new name, he argued, was "meant to represent the people of God, either those immediately dwelling with him in glory, or those on earth walking according to his commandments." And on April 26, 1838, the Lord revealed to Joseph Smith the final name: "For thus shall my church be called in the last days, even The Church of Jesus Christ of Latter-day Saints. Verily I say

unto you all: Arise and shine forth, that thy light may be a standard for the nations."

Despite our official name, only recently, thanks to President Nelson, have we begun to more fully embrace the term *Latter-day Saint* again. I wonder if one reason the term Mormon as a self-identifier became so widespread was a lingering cultural discomfort in claiming the identity of *saint*, latter-day or otherwise. *A wretch like me, a saint? And certainly not my elders quorum president!* Even though we, like Protestants, have tried to reclaim the New Testament meaning of saints as all the members of the body of Christ, the Catholic definition still prevails in our imagination. And after all, how many people have you known in your life that you would unreservedly proclaim a capital-S Saint? In my case, probably just one, my grandmother, St. Betty Jo Davis of Orem, the patron saint of stray animals and people, someone whose love was so pure and unconditional that a single conversation could provide healing for a lifetime.

But how can ordinary disciples become more comfortable embracing our identity as saints? Let me offer one possibility. The Tyndale Bible Dictionary defines *saints* as "the people of the coming age." As followers of Jesus, we are called to bring the future kingdom of God into the present. As Paul urges, saints are not people who should "conform to this world," but instead be willing to be set apart, to engage in the work of transforming it through love. To be a saint is to be a bridge between our time and the time of fullness.

Consider the many ways Christians throughout history have brought God's kingdom nearer. In opposition to Roman culture, early Christians condemned infanticide, gave women leadership roles and respect, and proclaimed the inherent value and equality of every individual. In the middle ages, Christians established universities, hospitals, orphanages, and houses for the poor. In the nineteenth century, Christian activists led the fight against slavery and child labor, while in the twentieth, Jesus's teachings on nonviolence

SAINT BETTY JO OF OREM

inspired Indian independence, the American Civil Rights movement, and the peaceful dissolution of the Soviet Union. In every case, the saints transcended the problems and limitations of the temporal by embracing and partnering with the eternal.

The challenge and thrill of sainthood is to perceive and respond to the specific crises of your own age with living faith and radiant love. And heaven knows there are many latter-day needs that Latter-day Saints can address: loneliness and despair, poverty and addiction, polarization and fear, environmental destruction, and above all, a civilization-wide spiritual famine that cries out for relief.

But problems of this magnitude can't be overcome by a single great Saint. Instead, we need a great many ordinary saints, striving together to live and model a radically different form of life, one rooted in a love beyond reason. A covenant community that seeks to nurture, embody and share the fruits of God's kingdom: peace, compassion, forgiveness, justice, freedom, mercy, belonging. We become the saints the world needs as we link arms with our brothers and sisters in Christ, bear one another's burdens, and together create hospitals of holy healing.

In this process of attending and responding to the world, we become the visible display of the infinite goodness of God. Our prayer is that the writing and art in this issue provide glimpses of that goodness and blueprints for the coming kingdom. *Come, come, ye saints, no toil nor labor fear, but with joy wend your way.* ✸

# A CHURCH THAT IS REAL

*Walking the Path of Most Resistance*

MELISSA WEI-TSING INOUYE

S A YOUTH I ALWAYS HAD QUE-stions about faith, but I did not dwell on them seriously until I went to university. At Harvard College, I wandered happily in the library stacks, surrounded by books analyzing events, ideas, and problems that had never before crossed my mind. I learned to interrogate an idea and poke hard at its soft spots. This was mostly fun. However, when I poked at my own beliefs, especially in the light of new things I was learning about my church's history, I felt tender and a bit at a loss.

At Harvard, I became acquainted with Laurel Thatcher Ulrich, a renowned professor and beloved mentor for Latter-day Saint students. When I read her 1986 essay, "Lusterware," reprinted in the spring 2024 issue of *Wayfare*, it made a deep impression on me.[1] "Lusterware," Laurel explained, was a type of ceramic dishware popular in the late eighteenth century. It was plated with a platinum film so as to resemble solid silver, but if you dropped it, it would fall to pieces like ordinary crockery. In an Emily Dickinson poem, lusterware was a metaphor for disillusionment—a shining, supposedly solid thing which fell and

unexpectedly shattered on "the stones at [the] bottom of my mind." Warning against a "lusterware" view of what we then called Mormonism, Laurel recalled one time in which a distressed young person in the middle of a faith crisis came to her worrying that the Church was perhaps only ninety percent (instead of one hundred percent) divine. To this, Laurel responded, "If you find any earthly institution that is ten percent divine, embrace it with all your heart."

This idea sent shockwaves across my mind. Growing up, the gospel message drummed into my head was the message of the hundred percent. To my young self the stock phrases "I know the Church is true" and "the fulness of the gospel" referred to my church's complete sufficiency and comprehensiveness. Church leaders were always divinely directed, whether it was a bishop giving dating advice or a general authority criticizing the theory of evolution. This hundred percent outlook meant that there was no room for error, no possibility of contradiction, and no need to improve. In this view, the Church was the best of all possible worlds. Everything was as it should be, and should have been.

# But there are not two Churches and I am not divided. There is one Church, and I claim it as my own, ashamed of what is shameful and proud of what is praiseworthy.

This is why Laurel's suggestion to treasure a venture that was less than "one hundred percent divine" was both provocative and lifesaving. As a university student, the "all or nothing" framework left me with a faith crisis as I learned about Church history, including past Church leaders' flaws and fallibility. Clearly, there were times when Latter-day Saints had made mistakes with long-lasting and harmful repercussions. As I struggled to readjust my worldview, Laurel's example of embracing both divine direction and human limitation was a lifeline.

The Church that is true is a Church that is real, and a Church that is real is a Church that embodies contradictions and contrasts, which characterize the nature of reality itself. God's plan does not call on us to escape life's messiness by retreating to a bubble free of doubt and conundrum. Instead, our Heavenly Parents have given us the opportunity to struggle mightily with life's puzzles, thereby exercising our divine capacity. We reason and rage. We stumble, and correct course. We learn to be unshaken. We learn to bend.

The Church that is real is a Church that is patriarchal, hierarchical, and USA-centric. It is a Church with a history that, like its wider host society, includes racism, sexism, and nationalism.[2] It is a Church that shapes a distinctive "culture region" in the American Intermountain West known for conspicuous consumption and religious elitism. It is a Church in which some men in positions of ecclesiastical power have used that power to abuse others emotionally or sexually, in egregious violation of the Lord's instructions for righteous authority. It is a Church founded by Joseph Smith Jr., who instituted a radical new system of marriage, and who concealed some of his additional marriages from his first wife Emma, for whom plural marriage was an excruciating ordeal.[3]

The Church that is real is also a Church that engaged in radical redistribution of wealth and communitarian economics. It teaches a theology of humankind's literal divine nature as beloved children of a Heavenly Father and Mother. All over the earth it facilitates the formation of local communities with their own distinctive cultures. It is a Church that unites rich and poor, north and south, women and men in sacred covenants to take upon themselves the name of Christ and mourn with those that mourn. It is a Church that calls people to serve, regardless of their caste or occupation, and obliges them to develop their capacities and become blessings in the lives of others. It is a Church whose founder, Joseph Smith Jr., had a radical new vision of eternity and humankind's limitless potential to make enduring connections and bring forth good fruits.

Looking at the previous two paragraphs, if some were to read only the first they might conclude that I am an "anti-Mormon" being critical. If some were to read only the second they might call me an "apologist" pushing a rosy ideal. But there are not two Churches and I am not divided. There is one Church, and I claim it as my own, ashamed of what is shameful and proud of what is praiseworthy. My loyalty does not arise out of a calculation that the pros outweigh the cons, but out of reciprocity. In addition to the gift of Christ's atonement, which he gives freely to all, I owe a debt to my sisters and brothers. Fellow Latter-day Saints have taught me to want to be good, protected me from danger, and helped make real the things I wanted to be true but could not see.

For me, one significant cost of this repayment is not merely time, money, meals, and mileage, but cognitive and emotional effort. Why must I labor to contextualize the racist language sometimes recorded in the Book of Mormon, our precious and holy book of scripture? When will the fundamental truth that women and men are spiritual equals created in the image of a Heavenly Mother and Heavenly Father, with the same potential to lead, teach, and bless the lives of their fellow beings, be meaningfully reflected in institutional Church decision-making structures? How do I maintain my faith in living prophets and apostles when history shows that over time, teachings sometimes change and contradict themselves? At one time in our early history plural marriage was elevated above monogamous marriage, but now it is grounds for discipline (unless it is for time and all eternity in the temple). At one time, using birth control would damn you and your posterity to the third and fourth generations, but now it's not a problem. At one time, some Church leaders wrongly depicted Black people as "fence-sitters" in the pre-existence, but as of 2015 this has been officially disavowed (though it lingers on some Church members' family bookshelves). If the Church is true, why can't it be "right" all of the time? Sometimes I grow weary of always having to explain! To compensate! To wait patiently! To put things "on the shelf"! The—damn—shelf—is—full!

For me, the long-term solution to these frustrations is not to abandon thoughtful reflection by compartmentalizing spiritual life. Some feel that critical thinking and deep faith do not mix. But for me, life with God in it comes as a whole package. If I can't make sense of my Latter-day Saint belief and practice in relation to all experience and all knowledge, then it isn't worth the effort. True, there are many things which we cannot know. But some basic paradigm should be reliable and worthy of wholehearted trust.

Nor do I feel that I personally would be happier, in the long run, abandoning the Church with the intent of moving on to a dissonance-free lifestyle. In today's world, nearly all of the institutions, organizations, and global structures within which we make our lives are ethically compromised, devilishly complex, and muddied by human error and apathy. To thrust in one's sickle in any of these places, cultivating a good harvest and eradicating weeds, is not only to improve that part of God's vineyard but also to develop capacity and experience for acting in the wider world. Time and again, my Latter-day Saint sisters and brothers have lent me inspiration and strength to bring to pass what I want, and need, to accomplish in my community, profession, country, and planet.

When someone asked Jesus what was most important, he responded: first, love God with all your heart, soul, mind, and strength; second, love your neighbor as yourself. On these two

*James Rees*

commandments, he said, hang all the law and the prophets.

I am thankful that Jesus included "mind" and "strength" as ways to love God. To engage the mind in the project of faith is not a slippery deviation, but a consecrated contribution to God's kingdom. Such intellectual engagement requires effort (strength). Here Jesus is putting this kind of effort on par with humans' other capacities of emotional, spiritual, and intellectual power. Perhaps effort is valuable in and of itself. As we seek to obey the two great commandments within the Church, we

*James Rees*

practice unselfishness and persistence. We never get it just right, but it is honest work.

Honest intellectual work sometimes leads to cognitive dissonance. That is to say, when one becomes aware of contradictions in what Latter-day Saints believe and do, particularly when these contradictions uniformly invoke divine authority, a murmur develops in the mind which is hard to ignore. For me, at one point, this cognitive dissonance was a deal-breaker. To my way of thinking, I was a smart, rational person who could not belong to an incoherent, irrational religion. Now, however, I have come to believe that cognition is not the most important aspect of being human. Like digestion, cognition is an essential process. Without it we would die. Yet in order to live in accordance with the reality of who we are as children of God (i.e., in accordance with truth), what is most vital is for us to pursue being good, as God is.

The Apostle Paul argued that even if someone had tremendous spiritual power, enough to prophesy, but had not charity, that person's utterances would be empty as a "tinkling cymbal." Even someone who understood all mysteries and knowledge, but had not charity, he said, was "nothing." Spiritual and intellectual power are not substantial in and of themselves, but only in relation to others. They help us to love God, but unless we also employ them to love our neighbors and "our strangers" they are for naught.

When I ask, "Which is harder: to say something smart and critical about Latter-day Saint practice, or to care for others as much as I care for myself?" the answer is clear. When I ask, "With what do I need more divine help: becoming smarter and more knowledgeable, or becoming kinder and more able to help others?" the answer is clear. When I ask, "Am I better positioned to accomplish God's work by myself, or in the company of fellow travelers?" the answer is clear. For me, being a Latter-day Saint and participating in the mission of the Church is an opportunity to be more: to develop greater capacity to love; to know and serve; to enlist help. It is an opportunity to do something difficult but worthwhile.

I have friends who have decided to do good as individuals, without an organized religious community. Sometimes I envy their escape from the constant struggle to sort between divine fiat and tyrannical culture, godly practice and rote process. More often, however, I rejoice in my many sisters and brothers, in our humble collective search for the divine.

I also have friends who have left the Latter-day Saints and joined another religious community unencumbered by the "baggage" peculiar to our own faith and history. I respect their sense of integrity and feel that God consecrates their worthy work. In my professional study of religious traditions, particularly Buddhism, I have learned profound spiritual truths. I have also learned that all religious traditions have their own human histories, contradictions, and reasons for regret.

For myself, I choose to be a Latter-day Saint because I love our covenants: to God, to each other, and to the world. I love the baptismal covenant to bear one another's burdens, the sealing covenant to make human love everlasting, the temple covenant to consecrate our time and talents in establishing a Zion in which there are no poor among us. I rejoice in the power of these covenants to bind us across the world, to make us equal as we stand before God, to convert hope into solemn promises. I believe that these Latter-day Saint covenants are true, which is to say I believe God's power truly inhabits them, and through this power things which were otherwise impossible become possible.

In early 2017 I was diagnosed with colon cancer. I had surgery to remove the tumor in June. During the weeks of recovery, I remained home by myself in New Zealand while my husband and children went to the United States to visit our family. One night a sister from Relief Society, Sister Samuelu,[4] knocked on the door. She was a Samoan woman who spoke English as a second language. She stepped into my kitchen with a bunch of flowers. Her face, with its wrinkles and sags, and her voice, worn down with use, reminded me of my Chinese grandmother. She chatted genially about the new investigator from Brazil, and her granddaughter who is on a mission in Australia, and how once the missionaries lived in a haunted house but how "they've just got to be brave." I thanked her for the time she had spent

## Yet in order to live in accordance with the reality of who we are as children of God, what is most vital is for us to pursue being good, as God is.

with my two younger children when she was their Primary teacher. She replied that in truth, she had been getting tired of Primary but felt that it was important for the kids to have a teacher who showed up. She gave me her phone number and told me to text her anytime.

As her visit seemed to be coming to a close, I thanked her and gave her a hug. Then, surprising me, she asked: "Can I leave you with a prayer?" "Sure, thank you," I said, sitting down again. For some reason, I didn't close my eyes all the way, but stared down at the floor. I felt as if I were an observer. At that time of anxiety and pain, I didn't really know what to expect from prayers. I was afraid that beyond "Thy will be done," there was nothing to say.

Sister Samuelu said: "Bless Melissa so that she can live to take care of her kids." With great eloquence, she invoked blessings on my body, my spirit, the house, my children and husband far away. The specific words escape me, but I remember a feeling of deep, settling calm. I felt as if I could feel my blood vessels widening and my lungs expanding. This is what the presence of the Holy Spirit feels like to me. Sister Samuelu hadn't laid her hands on my head, but she had indeed blessed me, as did our Latter-day Saint foremothers in the nineteenth and twentieth centuries.

At this lonely juncture in my life, I was blessed by an older Samoan woman who has never made an academic argument, who but for the Church would never have come into my life to teach my children and minister to me. Her prayer said what I had been afraid to say and asked what I had been afraid to ask. It is frightening to face a life-threatening illness and wonder whether God intends for you to make it to the other side. You feel foolish pleading for your life, because it's quite possible that God has already seen that this will go nowhere. But if someone else makes

> **We, Latter-day Saints all over the world who labor to build Zion, are ordinary people with ordinary shortcomings. We regularly fail to live up to the measure of our divine callings. Nevertheless, God is real, and patient, and among us.**

this plea on your behalf, you feel not presumptuous, but grateful, and receiving. Through Sister Samuelu, I felt God's power and care in my mind, my heart, and my body.

Sometimes we need others to plead with God alongside us. This is not because God responds to popularity contests, but because sometimes individuals wrestling with mortality are just not up to the task. The Church's many structures, some of which I have experienced as teeth-gnashingly bureaucratic and subject to patriarchal control, are nevertheless designed to facilitate this sort of potentially transformative human interaction and intercession. Here, in the spaces between us, spring up fountains of living water.

Although they are irreducible to neat percentages, we can embrace both the human and the divine within the Church. We, Latter-day Saints all over the world who labor to build Zion, are ordinary people with ordinary shortcomings. We regularly fail to live up to the measure of our divine callings. Nevertheless, God is real, and patient, and among us.

It is genuinely painful to encounter un-Christlike behavior not only "in the world" but also within one's own Church and its history. But since I myself am a regular source of un-Christlike behavior, this pain is something I must own. I must have the integrity to take responsibility for what needs fixing and put my shoulder to the wheel. Just like volunteering to vacuum carpets and empty trash in the meetinghouse, there are ways to volunteer time and energy to repair and renew the living structures of my Church.

The work of living with contradiction and tension is also something I must own. While it can be a relief to associate only with like-minded individuals with "correct" educational backgrounds, political views, class values, and theological inclinations, it is also a sort of prison—a sanitized separation from the fecund soil of humanity in which God wants us to spread our roots. If our Heavenly Parents had intended for everyone to think alike and to follow the same path back to them, they could have endorsed Lucifer's plan. Instead they gave us the power of agency, which is the power to make terrible mistakes and cause lasting damage. But it is also the power to be brave, to be wise, to extend the self, and to be a true healer.

The fundamental reality of humanity is that our values and assumptions are rooted in the diverse circumstances into which we were born, and we disagree deeply about what is good and true. The Church is not a solution for the problem of diversity, but a preserve within which to practice diversity's values. It is a gritty sandbox within which we bump against each other and become more polished. It is a place with enemies to love, peace to make, and cause for meekness. In this our teacher is the Holy One who ministered in the shadow of imperial power, associated with tax collectors and centurions, met with despised outcasts, and taught people in their own lands and languages. His was always the path of most resistance.

The path as a Latter-day Saint in pursuit of Zion is not always an easy path, but ease is not its purpose. Here I have found people to love and people who love me. Here I have ample cause to rejoice, to grieve, to act, and to be still. Here I am becoming more than I was, and more as I hope Christ has invited me to be. ✴

1.   Laurel Thatcher Ulrich, "Lusterware," *Wayfare*, Spring 2024, 175–79.

2.   M. Russell Ballard, "The Trek Continues!," *Ensign*, November 2017, 106.

3.   "Plural Marriage in Kirtland and Nauvoo," Gospel Topics Essays, The Church of Jesus Christ of Latter-day Saints, accessed May 26, 2024.

4.   I've used a pseudonym.

MELISSA WEI-TSING INOUYE

1979 - 2024

# BREAKING MY FACE

*Some Thoughts on Joy*

ROBBIE TAGGART

PIERRE TEILHARD DE CHARDIN wrote that "everything that rises must converge."[1] He imagines ascending in love and wisdom until we find ourselves at the summit of existence surrounded by those devotees of goodness from all walks of life who have climbed the same radiant peak, delighted by the community of the consecrated. Lehi intimated that everything that will ultimately rise must first fall: "Adam [and Eve] fell that [humanity] might be, and men [and women] are that they might have joy."[2] In order to participate in the communion of the joyous, we must begin below. Sometimes the ascent to joy from our mortal fallings demands fierce determination and grace.

As a teenager of modest means, I often found myself with my friends in the backcountry of our local mountains on a snowy afternoon, scaling a slope to catch a free ride on our snowboards. The winter sun multiplies its brilliance as it reflects off the expanse of a white mountainside. An invigorating peace breathes through those high places. One day, after almost a foot of snow had fallen in the valley, we drove up the canyon with our boards. We laughed in the light as we hiked through knee-deep drifts, then we rode the fresh powder to the base of the glen. The ethereal feeling is difficult to describe, but it lies somewhere between floating among cumulus clouds and catching hold of the coattails of God. You feel invincible and weightless.

After our first run, my friend suggested we climb to a small cliff we had jumped before. It was a slight escarpment of eight feet or so that merged at the bottom with the slanting mountainside so that once you landed you could continue riding downhill. Infused with the ecstatic sense of buoyancy from our powder ride, I hiked to a spot above the cliff and headed straight down without much carving to manage my descent. When I hit the lip of the jump, I lost control and didn't land with my board parallel to the ground as I intended. I don't remember too much about that fall, but my board turned perpendicular to the slope and sunk into the soft powder where it stuck fast. My feet planted, but my face kept falling. My knee came up to greet my face with an abundance of enthusiasm. I think I can still remember the sound of the crunch. When I came to my senses, my friends were searching the bloody snow for my teeth.

In time we found the teeth still inside my mouth, dangling from the roots hanging from my broken maxilla, the bone that normally holds

# God who sings the sunrise new each morning brings the dance to our eyes as well: an awakening with this outpouring of grace—an arising.

your teeth in place. I refer to that as the day I broke my face. I broke my nose and my jaw. My lower teeth went through my lip—all the way through. One trembling and loyal friend shot down the mountain on his board in search of help. He found a snowmobiler who came as far up the mountain as he could. Two other friends carried me between them and helped load me on the back of the snowmobile. I remember apologizing for bleeding on the man's coat. He told me to please not worry for blessed heaven's sake and to hold on. He took me to a ranger station. The ranger called an ambulance and provided first aid. I remember the long wait for that ambulance as bloody paper towels accumulated at my feet. The shock wore off. When the paramedics arrived, they gave me an injection of something wonderful and thick which carried me off into beautiful oblivion.

I awoke in the hospital after reconstructive and plastic surgery (I often tell my students that stunning looks like mine don't come naturally), and my parents took my puffy face home to rest. I couldn't eat for weeks, instead shooting instant breakfast shakes down my throat with a water bottle. To fix my jaw, the orthodontist installed a device that might have been invented by Dante himself to punish the purveyors of orthodontia. It was called a Herbst appliance. It was essentially two metal, telescoping bars on the insides of my mouth to keep my jaw straight as it healed and to push my teeth forward. It dug into my cheeks. It came unhinged if I laughed or yawned, and then it would either get stuck open, making it impossible to close my mouth, or it would separate and stab the roof of my mouth. Life was deluxe.

The orthodontist promised that the charming contraption would be removed after six months. Over a year later, it was ready to come out. As I sat in the chair, mouth agape, the orthodontist began digging around with something that looked like pliers pulled from a toolbox. He paused mid-twist and asked if I had premedicated. Nobody had told me I needed to take amoxicillin, but the orthodontist assured me it was important and offered to write me a prescription. It seems a small thing in retrospect, but I was a teenage boy with testosterone raging through my lithe frame, and I was frustrated. I thought I would go fill the prescription and return within minutes, but the doctor told me to set an appointment to return. When the smiling receptionist told me it would be ten days before they could get me back in, I began seeing red. I had heard of blind fury, and my vision began to blur. I stalked out the door, trying to slam it behind me, but it was one of those pneumatic doors that can't be banged shut. I slammed my car door and drove home yelling at all the other cars I couldn't see through the rage blur, yelling at heaven, yelling at the orthodontist. It was only ten days, but it felt sempiternal to me.

When I got home, my perennially kind mother opened the door from the house to the garage to celebrate with me the removal of this piece of metal. She was unprepared for the feral creature that greeted her, snarling and howling. "What's the matter, Robb?" she asked. "Look in my mouth!" I yelled. I stormed past her and stomped to my bedroom, where I searched for something to break. I unplugged the computer monitor on my desk and began carrying it outside. My mother followed behind me, asking tentatively, "Robb, what are you doing?" I could still hear her baffled, "Robb? Robb?!?" as I swung the computer around my head by the cord and smashed it into the concrete patio. It shattered with a satisfying explosion, scattering glass and plastic. Can it be that my mother asked if that made me happy? I can't remember. But I needed to go for a walk. I remember growling and grumbling at cars as I walked toward a corner store not far from my house. As I went in to purchase

*Nicholas Stedman*

a fruit drink—a kiwi-strawberry Mistic, specifically—I was muttering my incoherent frustration, "Premedicate . . . Nobody told me . . . Ten days . . . ."

There in the corner store I paid for my drink, my hands shaking in anger. I opened the bottle and looked at the underside of the lid where I found the following message grinning back at me: "Happiness is a decision."

Two quick options flicked through my mind: either I hurl the bottle through the store window, shouting, "Happiness this!!" or I surrender my anger to humor. A humor laced with exquisite irony—a divine humor, the kind that makes a comedy of the bitterest tragedy. A vision entered my mind of God, beaming from ear to ear, calling over an angel in heaven, handing over the bottle of kiwi-strawberry Mistic and saying, "Please get this to that grumpy boy down there." I imagined the angel maneuvering the drink into place just before I grabbed it. I began to laugh. "Happiness is a decision." Fallen things rising in joy. Every day, life asks whether we want the way of gladness or some other way. Ascend the peak. Greet the joyful.

Joy is our inheritance as children of Heavenly Parents who delight in our existence. Heber C. Kimball affirmed, "I am perfectly satisfied that my Father and my God is a cheerful, pleasant, lively and good natured Being. Why? Because I am cheerful, pleasant, lively and good natured when I have His Spirit. . . . He is a jovial, lively person and a beautiful man."[3] God's joyfulness is our birthright, but we use our agency to live in the gift. Paul makes joy a verb: "We joy for your sakes before our God."[4] Joying is something we deliberately enact. We live the gladness of God.

I have learned that there is a method to choosing happiness. And joy comes more easily to some than to others. Researcher Sonja Lyubomirsky acknowledges that genetics play an important role in our "happiness set point," noting that 50 percent of our happiness is genetically determined, 100 percent is circumstantial, and 400 percent derives from intentional activity. But she affirms that "just because your happiness set point cannot be changed doesn't mean that your happiness level cannot be changed."[5] We can choose to practice gratitude, mindfulness, deepening relationships, compassion, and service. In short, we can practice choosing happiness.

Thomas Merton writes, "No despair of ours can alter the reality of things, or stain the joy of the cosmic dance which is always there. . . .

*Nicholas Stedman*

We are invited to forget ourselves on purpose, cast our awful solemnity to the winds and join in the general dance."[6] Sometimes I wonder, what would happen if God started laughing? A depth—a resonance—as clear and as ebullient as a river, so deep and so joyous we could barely swim in it. Awash with laughter, we'd splash in God's mirth. What if God started singing again, "Let there be light"? And we, oh loves, like Lazarus would wake up clear-eyed and refreshed, able to see as we are seen and sing as we are sung. God who sings the sunrise new each morning brings the dance to our eyes as well: an awakening with this outpouring of grace—an arising. What if God started dancing? And the whole world, no longer stooped in stupor, joined the bright dance, remembering we worship Joy. Reinhold Niebuhr asserts, "Humor is a prelude to faith; and laughter is the beginning of prayer."[7] There could be more joy in our worship, more laughter in our prayers. Rather than wringing our hands that the cart is toppling, we might dance like David before the radiant ark of the covenant.

Sometimes the joy chooses you. When he was three years old, my son Oliver and I were at the park playing together. I took a stick and wrote his name in the sand. Then he started dictating letters to me and I would write them: "O. G. F. E. F. O. What does that say?" "Ogfefo." "Is that a real word?" "I think you just invented it." His eyes got big, "So I own it!" "Yeah, you own it. It's all yours." He spelled a bunch of others. He was getting excited, "I own five words!" He was fairly hopping about. Then he spelled, "FEO. What does that say?" "Feo." "Is it a real word?" "Well, not in English, but it's a word in Spanish." "Oh, so I don't own it. The Spanish people own it." Raise your arms and give thanks, grinning. The joy chooses you.

To choose joy is not to live in blindness to the anguish of human suffering, but it is to determine not to be undone by the pain that abounds and to strive to see the golden thread of beauty that persists in our darkness. Once I received a phone call late in the evening from a friend. I could barely decipher through his grief-choked words that he wanted me to come to the hospital. When I arrived, this giant of a man fell sobbing into my arms. "He's not going to live," he said. He and his wife were expecting their second child, a son. She was in the next room, about to give birth to this baby boy who would not live more than an hour according to doctors. He had no kidneys. We cried and prayed together. When the baby came gasping into this world, holding on to life through his mom's umbilical cord, my friend took his son into his hands, and with a small group of men who loved this man and this boy, blessed the tiny infant. He tearfully gave the baby his own name, expressed love and gratitude for his birth and his existence, begged him to remember the family, to watch over them as he passed back into a life other than this one, and was silent. Baby James lived an hour and a half. His life was defined by love. Could there be a kernel of joy to be found

**To choose joy is not to live in blindness to the anguish of human suffering, but it is to determine not to be undone by the pain that abounds and to strive to see the golden thread of beauty that persists in our darkness.**

and planted in the communion of those who gathered in love? Is the beauty of connection a source of our gladness?

Are love and joy the same thing? Or at least close relatives? There were small moments of gladness that night, the products of a mother's fierce faith and a father's gentle hope. When James passed away, this baby's father asked us to give him, the father, a blessing. We laid hands on his head and expressed love and gratitude and hope, and we promised joy. As I drove home alone, I wept. I wept for sorrow, yes, but also for the sacred privilege of witnessing in two short hours two holy transitions: from light to love to light again. The twin miracles of entering and exiting this remarkable sphere of existence where we are that we might have joy. His brief life was charged with heartache and hope and holiness intermingled and interwoven, like the life of Christ: a God made man for an instant. A God who came to experience all our sorrows and sanctify them into wisdom, compassion, and growth. They say that those who die and return to life long for death again, yearning to drink light again—to taste color. But I can imagine this bright beautiful boy stepping from that circle of love back into the light of divine love and longing too—yearning for the feel of father's hands and mother's lips, the mortal sound of sister's laugh. Oh, we ache because we love. And we hope, eternally we hope that fallen things will rise again. That joy will have the final word. That seeds planted will one day shoot up as majestic trees ripe with fruit. That sorrow comes forth from the grave as something else entirely. That nothing bad is permanent. That only joy is eternal.

Beyond the cliffs that break our faces and the deaths that break our hearts, there are, of course, minor falls. Several years ago, I sat on the front porch contemplating the songlessness of entropy, the way the weeds creep and crush and encroach on my garden, my lawn, my flowerbed; the way the messes multiply and replenish in a family with five children. There's a certain dark miracle there in the relentless march of chaos and mayhem. It can sink into the soul and weigh you down.

But here's the point: That late summer afternoon, I looked up to see the stumbling, toddling, mad amble of my beautifully round fourth-born making her way across the grass, barefoot as a Carmelite, holding the hands of her two oldest siblings who gazed at her with reverent attentiveness. She was not yet two years old. This small child has oceans in her blue eyes. There are constellations and congregations of solemn clouds swirling behind her piercing glance. Ellie crouched at the edge of the green lawn to examine a rock. She made a wondering sound. The three older children all joined her in her genuflection toward the stone. They each touched it in turn with gentle affection. Then Ellie shot up and pointed exuberantly. The neighbor dog had come wandering into her consciousness. The children admired with her. She bent for a snail. They dropped to their knees. And I wanted to join them. Isaiah says that in the Millennium, when there is peace among all creatures, when the wolf and the lamb bound recklessly down grassy slopes, joyously united, and the lion and the ox share a communal feast of straw, that a little child shall lead them. I wanted to follow this child into a world of miracles, a world of wonder, light, and joy. My sinking heart began to lift inside my old dad chest, began to soar away from the pull toward despair and

**Can we listen for the sound of God laughing and watch for the joy at the heart of existence? Everything that falls must rise. Everything that rises will converge in the joy of God. Even Christ was planted in the earth before bursting forth from the grave, radiant to save.**

discouragement and to rise toward something sacred, toward joy. Joy is the light beneath all darkness, the music at the heart of all silences. We watch for it, listen attentively, choose gladness. "Joy is the infallible sign of the presence of God."[8] We can see God. Here. Now. In this moment. And the joy will come.

Can we listen for the sound of God laughing and watch for the joy at the heart of existence? Everything that falls must rise. Everything that rises will converge in the joy of God. Even Christ was planted in the earth before bursting forth from the grave, radiant to save. Come find me on resurrection morning. I'll be sitting on my front porch, joying. Then we'll rise, together. ✳

1. Pierre Teilhard de Chardin, *The Future of Man* (New York: Image Books/Doubleday, 2004), 186.

2. 2 Nephi 2:25.

3. "Remarks," *Deseret News*, February 25, 1857.

4. 1 Thessalonians 3:9; see also Romans 5:11; 2 Corinthians 7:13; Colossians 2:5; and Philippians 2:17–18.

5. Sonja Lyubomirsky, *The How of Happiness* (New York: Penguin, 2007), 39, 57.

6. Thomas Merton, *Thomas Merton, Spiritual Master* (New York: Paulist Press, 1992), 256.

7. Robert McAffee Brown, ed., *The Essential Reinhold Niebuhr: Selected Essays and Addresses* (New Haven, CT: Yale University Press, 1986), 49.

8. This quote is often attributed to Pierre Teilhard de Chardin. See, for example, Kent Millard, *The Gratitude Path: Leading Your Church to Generosity* (Nashville: Abingdon Press, 2015).

# IN SILENCE

JON
OGDEN

If poetry is words in the mouth,
this isn't it.

Is a prayer stuck on
a page a prayer at all?

How do you lift this bit of ink,
or this bit, to heaven?

Birds need bones of air
to take their flight —

Not the weight of caskets,
the wait without breath.

Why this tongue
if there is no bread?

Why these words if
they're not made flesh?

Alight in the dark —
morning sends new song.

Take your prayer
from God's open lungs.

# HOLY GESTURES

*Two Stories & A Poem*

ELIZABETH C. GARCIA

## ON UNICORNS

O N A SUNDAY LIKE ANY OTHER, I am scrambling after church to corral the littlest before she escapes from her class to run down the hall and through the chapel, which is usually occupied by penitents from the other ward. This of course means there is no post-meeting chit-chat, the kind my own mother would engage in for what seemed *hours* after church, prolonging our hunger and our scheduled date with the long hours of Sabbath boredom, during which, in true extrovert fashion, she would make one long phone call after another, the way a chain smoker lights his next cigarette from the butt of the last. My children, however, ended up with a mother who is all task, who wants only to finish the business of going and coming, of feeding, to seek the quiet hour in which they are temporarily occupied, and she can turn to her thoughts.

So when we've finally clattered and belted into the van and I've shifted to reverse, my ten-year-old daughter blurts out,

"Mommy, I found a unicorn in the Bible! It's in the scriptures! So I think they're actually real!"

I look back to see her bright eyes, her smile, her whole countenance shining with joy at this thought: white glitter-bodied horse, muscled with brilliance, its mane a rainbow, a whole spectrum of light shining from each shaft, the single swirling cone a bright pillar reaching up to the heavens with an angelic chorus harmonizing. *Yes, Virginia, there is a unicorn!*

Moments later, when she breaks down in tears, I realize—No, the right choice at that moment was *not* to point her to the footnote of Isaiah 34:7, which reads, "RE'EM, a wild ox," sending a ripple of disappointment through her, as if her body has missed one step descending a staircase. She buckles in a little grief, bursting out an angry, "How do I know what to believe"? She weeps at the trick words have played on her, at the loss of temporary hope—that the muscled density of animals could be corseted in a horse's lines like calligraphy, glowing with its own light—but also

*Jessica Sarah Beach*

at *me*. That in my need to teach, to correct, to point out truth and error—perhaps a tendency to live up to the smartest version of myself, rather than the kindest—I have taken the shine from her, put a kibosh on her naïveté, shut down the possibility of some future showdown of shame in which she discovers before her peers that she has been misled. I have ripped off the bandaid and found skin attached. Did I think to praise the real intent she brought to scripture? Did I consider the joy of the moment her heart leapt within her to see the word in print, the word of God, the proof, the incredulity—*ten years old, and I'm just now discovering this?* The excitement that carried her through the end of her class, that she kept like a pearl to show her mother and say, *Look what I found!*

I put the car back in park. The other two kids meanwhile have begun squabbling over Primary candy rights. So naturally I have to settle that dispute by digging through the random paraphernalia in my purse: Batman mask, sunscreen, garage door opener (so that's why the door keeps opening at random times!), fifty receipts, tampon wiggled free of its wrapper in the melee (I am lacking only an umbrella and coat rack!)—aha! One tender mercy, a Dove chocolate relic of a past Relief Society meeting—*Here son, all is now right with the world.*

Turning back to my daughter, I pass her a tissue, summon all my sympathies, and suggest (like I should have in the first place!) that when we get home, we'll look at the reference together and look up some things to answer her questions.

that he "breaketh the cedars of Lebanon" and "maketh them to skip like a calf [. . .] like a young RE'EM" (Psalm 29:5–6)

that he "exalts" our voices "like the horn of a RE'EM" and "anoints" us (Psalm 92:9–10)

What seems to pacify my daughter the most is the way the author kindly leaves room for speculation about the *possible* existence of some *extinct* creature that *might have* more closely resembled what my daughter envisioned (something from the Gospel of Lisa Frank). That a lack of evidence is not evidence of lack. That there is room for belief even in the face of what we circumscribe as fact, and once again, she has opened up to possibility, to her desires, to the idea that she can believe in the qualities of something, rather than requiring her idea of it to exist. That despite the thousands of years and shortcomings of language, some creature existed so mythic and powerful it captured the imagination of those psalmists, to compare to the power of Almighty God—something that had the strength of myth, something wild and unharnessed, something uncircumscribable; that its horns were a wild vehicle of prayer and desperation, a relic of what is unknowable about God, what is just out of reach, yet somehow reaches to us; that God's voice both breaks the cedars in us and grants us the joy of wild things, a joy we cannot yet comprehend; that he can raise even our voices to that of myth, in a way which sanctifies us—*Daughter, who could refuse to exult over this?*

But by now, her expression of curiosity and angst has waned to mere tolerance. Her eyes wander, distracted. That one magic moment when my child has opened herself to knowledge has closed like a snack cabinet. *She's ready to go. She's ready to eat.* She's ready to go find other ways to entertain herself, which she hopefully won't describe in years to come as "hours of Sabbath boredom." And I am the one changed. Captive to my thoughts. Pondering the weak links in the chain of this poor and marvelous medium of language. ✳

This seems to appease her enough that I can get us home.

Later, when we Google "unicorns in the Bible," one of the first links is an LDS *Living* article, only five years old, detailing unicorn references in the KJV, and what the alternate translations indicate. (I'm imagining a similar fraught scenario that might have prompted this author to write the article.) We read:

that God "hears the strength of a RE'EM" (Numbers 23:22)

that he hears us "from the horns of RE'EM" (Psalm 22:21)

# WHAT THE WIND SAYS

*There are days when death*
*is nowhere in the background.*
—Li Young Lee

SUNDAY AFTERNOON, THE LAST day of April, my kids are watching scripture videos. Outside, the wind is tussling in the trees, the sun slanting to create a pool of shade, a clovered glade in our sloping backyard, and I decide: *Kids, dinner tonight is a picnic.*

We carry blankets down to the lawn and spread our snacks and sandwiches, listen to the ocean roar of the roiling branches towering over our yard, a great nunnery of trees hymning over us. The children share their strawberries with the bunnies, who fight over the tops, then pause to lick the juice from their paws, tracing halos over their heads.

We take a walk, and discover in the thick brambles of white flowers, not yet blackberries, growing over the fence, that honeysuckle has taken root and twined its way through the white bower, likely sprouted there from the vine I once dragged two blocks home, leaving my son, age three, to cry in the street, refusing to ride his tricycle, angry he was asked to do a hard thing.

The kids chase each other through the wide grassy yard, which just a year ago was a forest of dog fennel and brambles. They explored the back slope of forest just outside the fence, traipsing up to the road to skirt their way around the thick patch of thorns growing adjacent to the house.

They jump on the trampoline, their hair alive with electrons. Lydia, perceiving injury, gives herself over completely to the grief of being wronged by the world, throws her head back with a howl and lets loose all the demons competing within her for the last crumb of attention.

Her brother, meanwhile, smirks at the power he has to cause this apocalypse.

My eleven-year-old shows me her flips on the still rings, her dress collecting at her thighs, and I wonder how many more times she will feel this free before retreating into the cave of teenage angst.

My husband kisses the back of my neck.

What is the right word for the way the wind brings to the surface the inner turmoil of every silent thing, their incessant squirming, the way a child, age five, cannot hold still, must clap her

Jessica Sarah Beach

hands and sing while I'm trying to brush her tiny gems of teeth?

Years ago, I came across the idea that the description of "the spirit of God" that "moved over" the waters in Genesis was an incomplete translation of the Hebrew. *Ruach Elohim m're-chephet* translates to "the spirit/breath/wind of God hovers." But more than this: the "-phet" ending of the verb indicates that the subject—God—is female. Or as some interpret this—the part of God that is female. It is *Her* breath, *Her* wind that hovers. It is *Her* spirit that stirs in us, through us, carries with it our dissatisfaction, our need to escape, to wake us to what is alive in the blades of grass. That we too, created, are still full of life, making our Sabbath, again, delightful.

We discover the evidence of some giant rodent who has dug up an earthwork under our slide, the perfect shelter for his burrow, the hole a sign of what can any minute be lost to us—this present tense, this glorying in our bodies, in the natural world we ignore for the fraught internal one.

My daughter tells me they climbed the deer stand, felt the swaying of the wind and knew to descend, unsure of the tree's ability to hold them, or how far it could bend without breaking. ✳

# UNSPOTTED

ELIZABETH C.
GARCIA

What does it mean to keep
something holy? Like I tell
my five-year-old, don't
get that syrup in your hair?
Might as well say don't eat.
Don't play. Don't live today,
or you'll get dirty. And aren't
all our hands grubby?
What can you keep without
killing it? When we found
a snail on the drive, frozen
and brought it in to warm,
it thawed and swelled, each
cell yawned and stretched
slow as grass, its dank muscle
like a tongue caught between
desires—to lick, or articulate?
If only one is holy,
what are we here for?
What is sacred without
the body, what is devotion
without it utterly offered up
to what it was meant for?
My daughter returns to me
five times or more, for a kiss
follows her kisses each time
with a lick. To her, no animal body
is unhuman, no gesture unholy
if it is alive—how could I ever
dare unlive her?

# ATTENDING TO LIFE

ELIZABETH
OLDFIELD

WHEN I PINE FOR MY PHONE, I CAN feel it on my skin, a tingle akin to a lover walking into the room. Patricia Lockwood calls it "the portal," glowing with the promise of significance and connection. Smartphones act like the enchanted Mirror of Erised in *Harry Potter*, which shows us what our heart desires but never allows us to reach out and take it. Dumbledore tells Harry, after he's sat up all night gazing at it, "Men have wasted away before it, entranced by what they have seen, or been driven mad, not knowing if what it shows is real or even possible."

Perhaps I am especially susceptible to the lure of technological connection, unusually weak-willed, because I have sometimes felt like I am being driven mad. I have two young children and all too regularly have a phone in my hand when they are trying to talk to me. It always feels like something important, worth the moment of disconnection, but at a distance I can see that I am often just scrolling listlessly and restlessly. I have social media blockers on all my devices, which worked well until I discovered you could switch them off easily. They invented a locked mode; I learned to delete the blocker app. Now I download and delete my blockers multiple times a day, like an overeater hiding food from themselves and repeatedly opening the cupboard.

You might not associate this endemic distraction with sloth, but before there was sloth, there was acedia. Acedia is both the Latin word we now translate as sloth and for many centuries its precursor. It's not simple laziness but a richer, more capacious concept, difficult to translate. I also think it is endemic, the unnamed temptation of our times.

John Cassian, a fifth-century monk, described brothers with acedia experiencing

*bodily listlessness . . . as though he were worn by a long journey or a prolonged fast. . . . Next he glances about and sighs that no one is coming to see him. Constantly in and out of his cell, he looks at the sun as if it were too slow in setting.*

Listlessness, distraction, apathy, restlessness. A monk never called it this, but I recognize it most in my own life when I'm dawdling. Failing to settle to anything, craving something, trying to sate a snackishness I'm only semiconscious of. Time feels either baggy or tight. The opposite of flow.

The monks who first coined acedia called it the "noonday demon," the post-lunch slump when all the focus and energy of the morning has worn off. It wasn't originally seen as a sin in itself, more a state of mind to be avoided. Chaucer, in gloriously juicy Middle English, said it "for-sloweth and forsluggeth" anyone attempting to act.

Acedia leaves me pinging around like a pinball, a "forsluggish" one sometimes, but also like the monk popping restlessly in and out of her cell hoping for a visitor, or a notification. Too many of my days are lived in this scattered state. Acedia neuters my ability to do good in the world, or even just properly enjoy it.

I don't want to be a pinball. I want to be a plant.

With a concept this broad, there isn't one opposite, but I've come to believe that the antonym of acedia is attention. The etymological root of attention is stretching toward something, moving intentionally closer. Ideally, I would decide carefully what warrants my attention, which people, ideas, objects or projects have sufficient meaning and value for me to spend a part of my fleeting life attending to them. I would stretch towards those things that will help me be kinder, freer, more just. Things that bring me genuine joy. Primarily, for me, people and relationships, but also meaningful work, meaningful play, beauty, real rest.

No matter how many articles I've read about how tech companies manipulate us with dopamine hits and our Pavlovian response to

notifications (articles I've found via social media), it's easy not to see the full danger of it. We are so seduced by the convenience and gloss and repeated tiny emotional rewards for compliance that we don't recognize the opportunity cost. How rapidly our lives are passing with our minds resting primarily on matters only pixel deep.

*Seth Neilson*

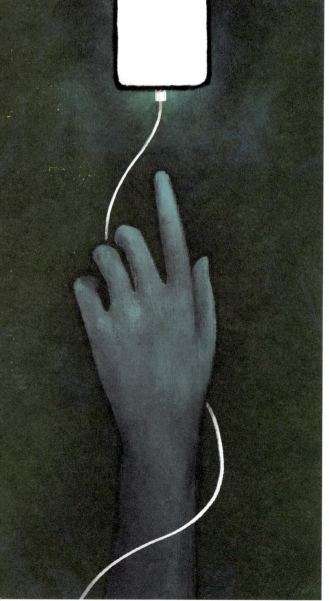

Philosopher and later Catholic martyr Thomas More wrote: "Many things know we that we seldom think on. And in the things of the soul, knowledge without remembrance little profiteth."

In other words, the things I "know" but fail to train my attention on do me little good. I wanted to live primarily for relationships, but the war on my attention means I am often failing, forgetting to remember what I know. When I stop to notice it, I feel actual rage. It is hard enough to live a good life, to do the work, to grow, without

> **We are so seduced by the convenience and gloss and repeated tiny emotional rewards for compliance that we don't recognize the opportunity cost. How rapidly our lives are passing with our minds resting primarily on matters only pixel deep.**

a context that is actively working against those things. I have to remind myself that learning to attend to what is important has always been a part of wisdom paths, distraction always a hurdle to overcome. Monetizing and mining our attention has accelerated, but isn't brand-new. Dorothy L. Sayers summarized the messaging of advertising in 1933 as:

> Whatever you're doing, stop it and do something else! Whatever you're buying, pause and buy something different. Be hectored into health and prosperity! Never let up! Never go to sleep! Never be satisfied. If once you are satisfied, all our wheels will run down.

Sayers' exclamation marks help me recognize the artificial urgency, to feel in my body the way the messaging of our culture is fracturing my relationship to time. Go! Go! Go! Do! Do! Do! Shiny! New! Over here! Take your eyes off the people in front of you and keep moving. Don't stretch steadily and intentionally towards the most important things, but ping around responsively, because this whole engine is running off your distracted, restless hustle.

My culture is telling me, in a million different ways, to never be satisfied.

I want to be satisfied.

I want to stop pinging around and put my roots down deep. I need to learn to draw nourishment from the gifts I have already received, the relationships in front of me. I am taking back my time and my attention.

It was only in my thirties that I began fully recognizing the powerful resources my tradition offers in this quest. I have come to the conclusion that training attention and structuring time are the hidden genius of religions. Yes, they give ethical guidance and existential comfort, but the centuries-honed tools they offer are a pragmatic, applicable and sane response to the madness of distraction and hurry.

The Rule of St. Benedict, the urtext for monastic thought, implies that it is precisely a well-ordered rhythm of days that keeps distraction at bay. Acedia is presented as a disruption of rhythm, a bum note in the song of the hours. I love Abraham Joshua Heschel's term for disordered time: "the screech of dissonant days." I react badly to the idea of a schedule but a rhythm sounds inviting. When I'm living in rhythm, time feels less like a quarry or an enemy and more like a dance partner.

A few years ago I decided that if St. Benedict was right then ordering my time is part of how I tend to my soul. I've been attempting to beat back my endemic acedia with a range of spiritual practices (you could call them spiritual technologies) that the church has used for centuries, and to do it not in a burst of enthusiasm that I then lose a few weeks later, but over years. Much to my annoyance, repetition seems to be the key. Our novelty-obsessed culture is allergic to repetition, associating it with dullness and scarcity, but that is a problem. Research on neuroplasticity and the power of habit only confirms what religions have always taught—the repeated, committed choices we make day after day are the sum of who we become. This means our own Rule of Life, the way we structure our time (whether by accident or design), is one of the most important choices we can make.

All these practices, as I learn to use them properly and regularly, feel like a trellis. They are helping me train my attention on the connected relationships I say I want to define my life. I feel saner, calmer, more focused. Spiritually alive.

## DAILY RHYTHMS: PRAYER AND CONTEMPLATION

I try to start the day with some kind of prayer. I can't pretend to live a full monastic rhythm every day, though I do try—and usually succeed, now—in keeping reasonable boundaries around work and making time for rest and hospitality. It's the commitment of part of my morning to prayer and sacred reading, though, despite all my natural instincts, that has been most transformative. Several times a week it is with others in the chapel. Other days prayer might just be journaling my thoughts vaguely heavenward in bed. Often, alone, with our community or with the kids over breakfast, I use written prayers from a modern monastic community based in Northumberland.

One line lifted from the Psalms always stops my distracted thoughts in their tracks: "Teach us, dear Lord, to number our days, that we may apply our hearts unto wisdom."

A modern paraphrase might be: Teach us to take our lives, our time seriously. Help us apply our hearts, turn our attention, orient our desires to wisdom. Help us to really live.

Saying the same things regularly has the effect of writing and overwriting the words onto my consciousness, reminding me of and reorienting me to what I want this day to be about.

## DAILY RHYTHMS: SACRED READING

I also read the Bible in the morning. It's my founding text, the narrative I locate myself in. Its strange oblique stories act as a counterweight to the cultural soup I'm swimming in the rest of the

> **I have to remind myself that learning to attend to what is important has always been a part of wisdom paths, distraction always a hurdle to overcome.**

time. It never fails to provoke, inspire or infuriate me. I am currently reading the Bible with a group of friends. We call it "wild Bible study" because in reading and chatting together we are not after one right answer, not seeking to solve anything. I used to try to read it like this, not least because many Bible study notes do make it feel like the text is a puzzle to be solved, its vivid and dense language in need of putting into doctrinal boxes. I found that approach boring, so I stopped going to Bible studies. Now I don't worry that there are many things I don't understand, whole books and passages I don't know what to do with. I don't think either Bible reading or faith itself is about resolution. It is a lot more like poetry, drama or music, which any good teacher will tell you are not completely amenable to the question "But what does it mean?" I want only to keep tasting it, turning it up to the light like a crystal to see just how much it holds.

## WEEKLY RHYTHMS: SABBATH

On Friday night, roughly as my work day ends, I turn off my phone, my iPad and my laptop and light a candle. It's a precious moment of peace. Then I jump up, hunt down a housemate, thrust all my devices hurriedly into their arms and ask them to hide them and (this with slightly wild eyes) NOT give them back to me on pain of death for twenty-four hours.

Sometimes it works. Often it doesn't, because the way we have set up society means there is usually (what seems like) a very important reason to turn them back on. If I can't get said housemate to crack I just use my husband's phone. More recently, we've tried committing to doing this together, as a community, which has helped a bit. I still successfully manage twenty-four hours

off devices only about half the time, but the attempt every week feels important.

Tech sabbaths and digital detoxes, even half-arsed ones like mine, are a modern iteration of one of the oldest ideas in civilization. In the second chapter of the Hebrew Bible, itself one of the oldest documents we have, [God] undertakes six days of creative work and rests on the seventh. He blesses the day and declares it "holy."

Theologian Walter Brueggemann called the practice of sabbath an act of resistance. The word conjures French fighters, stylishly sabotaging Nazi infrastructure while smoking Gauloises. Imagining myself in a beret with red lipstick really helps when I attempt to turn off my phone for a day. It's certainly a more attractive image than the grey, dull associations most of us carry. Sabbath sounds to us like the shop closing early just when we've run out of milk. It sounds like restriction. Which it is. But it is also through restriction, liberation.

For most of the week, my value is in what I produce and what I consume. If I'm not careful, my main goal in a day becomes being impressive and competent, subtly signaling my status with the things I buy, say and post.

Sabbath is the opposite. It is a line in the sand. Today I am just a person, and a person is beyond price. Sabbath is about valuing, fighting for and fiercely guarding rest.

I have had to learn to choose rest in a culture that only really recognizes frantic work and exhausted, passive leisure, ideally consumed using the same screens we've been working on all day, produced by the same small number of global corporations. Despite being deeply convinced of my need for rest, sometimes the only way I can justify sabbath to myself is on a productivity basis. Jews, who have been persecuted and mocked partly for their observance of it, have had to do this over the centuries. The Romans (proto-neoliberals?) were contemptuous of it, believing it revealed laziness to have a day off a week. Philo, a first-century Jew, made the case that his community was more effective and productive because of their day off: "A breathing spell enables not merely ordinary people but athletes also to collect their strength with a stronger force behind them to undertake promptly and patiently each of the tasks set before them." Rabbi Joshua Heschel, though, condemns this justification, saying, "Here the Sabbath is represented not in the spirit of the Bible but in the spirit of Aristotle." For Jews and Christians, the sabbath is not designed to serve work, because love, not work, is our ultimate end. It always moves me that the sabbath command was given directly after the Exodus, to a nation that had until recently been enslaved for generations. There is a tenderness in mandating rest and play for traumatized people who had only ever known enforced labor.

Mandated time to rest seems a foreign notion now. It's become one of the few clear political intuitions I have: that it shouldn't be. Breaking time, and people, into ever flexible units of production is one of the strongest drivers of disconnection that we experience. I have come to see sabbath as central for my personal project of connection, with myself, with my family and community and with [God]. It's a relational reset every week, a bulwark against the instrumentalization of relationships and the commodification of time.

And rest is, fundamentally, about being human. About recognizing our limits when advertising tells us we are limitless. It requires intention, and working out what we do actually find restorative. It is going in the bath with a book for me (but not with an iPad), or gardening, or rollerblading, or puttering around charity shops without my phone. I need to not have access to the news or social media in order to rest.

It might seem counterintuitive to prescribe rest as a medicine for the sin that is often known as sloth, but I think it's right. Proper rhythms of real rest rather than passive leisure consumption make focus easier when we need to work, make it more likely we will find joy and flow in it when we do.

## WEEKLY RHYTHMS: LITURGY

The point of a liturgy is to continually direct our desires. They are heart-shaping technologies and they help create our character. No formation without repetition, the saying goes; we are what we repeatedly do.

Philosopher James K. A. Smith calls secular versions "cultural liturgies," and names going to a football game or a regular trip to the shopping

> The point of a liturgy is to continually direct our desires. They are heart-shaping technologies and they help create our character.

mall as examples. Both involve their own rituals. Smith's work has helped me see the power of repetition, ritual and image to form and orient me. It's made me more aware of how often I am mindlessly participating in liturgies that are shaping me in directions in which I have not consciously consented to go. And so I now see participating in church liturgy as a form of pushback, another little resistance. I am making a free(r) choice about what I want to shape me, what values and desires I want inscribed on my heart and mind. Particularly in a church that uses a small number of set texts again and again, as all Catholic and most Anglican churches do, the words can become deeply ingrained. This can sound dull and rote. Like most teenagers and young people, I spent a long season thinking only entirely spontaneous, "authentic" self-expression counted, including in prayer, and that all tradition and structure was deadening.

However, as I age I begin to see the value of regular (even, whisper it, sometimes mindless) repetition. Some days the words come alive and feel deeply sincere, my thinking is stretched and enriched by their beauty, and other days I say them out of habit, but they are always forming me. Every week I give at least part of my attention to a ritual that reminds me of the things I am in danger of forgetting. I use my body as well as my mind, standing and kneeling and sitting and singing. I often dance around at the back and have stopped caring about the curious glances. During the various Covid-related lockdowns and restrictions it was this singing and dancing I missed the most. My voice is nothing special, but belting a song with a hundred other people can't help but sound beautiful. I often cry. For an hour and a half I don't look at my phone, and when I come out my thoughts feel saner and steadier. ✳

BISHOP ROBERT BARRON

# THE GLORY OF GOD

*This is an excerpt from a 2023 address delivered at the Harvard Catholic Forum.*

**THERE IS NO HUMANISM ANYWHERE,** east or west, or across the ages, greater than Christian theology. I say that without fear of contradiction. Why? Because the goal of Christianity is not simply the political or economic liberation of human beings, not just the psychological amelioration of our condition—the ordinary goal of the Christian life is to become divinized. ¶ There's a great statement you find in almost all the church fathers: *Deus fit homo, ut homo fieret Deus.* "God became human, that we humans might become God." ¶ It's a staggering claim that God became one of us so that we lowly humans might become divinized. How is that possible? Because God's not competitive with us. He's not a supreme being who exists in an antagonistic relationship with creation. In Jesus, divinity and humanity come together without mixing, mingling, or confusion in mutual harmony. That's the grounds of Christian humanism, and I would argue there's none that could be greater than that.

There's no aspiration higher for humanity than divinization. ¶ So much of modern philosophy is predicated upon that view of a competitive, overbearing God who is a threat to human freedom and human flourishing. I say: that's an idol, a false God. Rather, the proper understanding of God gives rise to the sweetest sort of humanism. My hero here is St. Irenaeus of Lyon, the great second-century church father. He said, "The glory of God is a human being fully alive." God glories in our being fully human. ✳

*Jean Fouquet (Text & Image Design by Cole Melanson)*

# YE SHALL BE AS THE GODS

SHARLEE
MULLINS
GLENN

How far from Eden's shadow must we go?
foundlings banished, sick with nameless dread,
looking always backward, ne'er ahead,
longing for the lushness, for the flow
of Gihon's honeyed waters. Now we know.
Our seeing eyes perceive we were misled—
promised knowledge; given pain instead.
How far? How far from Eden must we go?
Blood-smeared, sweat-bleared we toil to bring forth fruit
from earth, from loin. Then what this sudden rapture?
From whence the breeze, and how so sweet the gall?
Surprised by Joy, we feel our souls uproot
and soar toward that holy armature
upraised in honor of the blessed fall.

*Published previously in Fire in the Pasture:* Twenty-first Century Mormon Poets, *edited
by Tyler Chadwick. Peculiar Pages, 2011, p. 187*

# THE *YES, AND* GOSPEL

*Love as Faithful Elaboration*

**GREG CHRISTENSEN**

*ES, AND* IS THE CARDINAL rule of improv comedy. It's a tool actors use to keep a scene running in front of a live audience. On stage, it goes like this: An actor throws out an unrehearsed scenario or idea. For example, "Wow! I've never seen so many stars in the sky!" The partner in the scene then has the responsibility to agree with and build on that comment. It might be something like, "I know. Things look so different up here on the moon."[1] Actors continue to build on each other's reactions, catalyzing each response with, *yes, and*—an agreement, and a contribution. Anything else brings the scene to a halt. As SNL veteran Amy Poehler explains, "When you're in an improv scene and someone comes in and says 'Doctor, the patient is ready,' and you say, 'I'm not a doctor. We're in Paris. Why are you holding that baguette?' We're a little stuck."[2]

*Yes, and* isn't just for comedy. The Second City, the improv theater where comedians like Bill Murray and Stephen Colbert got their starts, has a corporate education arm that teaches improv principles like *yes, and* for business. A brainstorming session is the corporate world's version of the improv stage. If a coworker suggests a new

pricing model, which of these responses do you think would be the most helpful?

"Yes, and we can test it against our current one to find efficiencies."

"I'm not sure that would work."

One is curious and open to possibilities. The other not only shuts down the conversation, it likely chills the enthusiasm of other participants.

*Yes, and* even works when it doesn't look like there's a solution. Imagine an employee seeking a raise from an employer who simply can't give one due to budget constraints. The employer can say, "We're not giving raises now. There's nothing I can do." Or she can say, "Yes, I know you deserve a raise, and even though it's not possible now, we should talk about it." *Yes, and* is about listening, validating, and making a path forward, not capitulating.

Some couples therapists encourage *yes, and* in their counseling, because it can help partners validate feelings and elevate difficult conversations into more positive and productive planes. Think of the tension in statements like, "We went over budget again!" or "You never help with the kids!" That tension is exacerbated with defensive responses like, "It's not my fault!" or "I work all day!" or "What am I supposed to do?" But a *yes,*

# We see *yes, and* throughout the scriptures, particularly when there's the potential for conflict.

*and* response that validates and builds can ease the tension and pave the way for positive conversation and cooperative action.

*Yes, and* has been indispensable to me as a creative director in advertising. Most of my career has been spent in rooms with art directors trying to build on each other's ideas. Years ago I was part of a team doing pro bono work for the National Parks Conservation Association. This isn't an exact transcript, but our *yes, and* thinking went something like this:

ART DIRECTOR: "What if we told people our National Parks need their support because they're so unique?"

COPYWRITER: "Yes, and we could highlight how irreplaceable they are."

ART DIRECTOR: "Yes, and it's not like we can just make new ones."

COPYWRITER: "Yes, and if we did, they'd be these ridiculously fake replicas."

ART DIRECTOR: "Yes, and can you imagine what blueprints for something like that would be?"

The final ads featured blueprints of a manufactured Delicate Arch, Yosemite Falls, and a sequoia with the headline, "It's not like we can make new ones." These never would have come into existence if I'd responded with, "No, I don't think that will work."

The more I use *yes, and*, the more I wish I'd been taught this thinking as a full-time missionary. I received all kinds of training on my mission. I went to mission prep classes hosted by my stake. In the Missionary Training Center, teachers paid special attention to developing skills like goal

*David Habben*

setting, building relationships of trust, and effective weekly planning. In the mission field we had regular district, zone, and mission conferences where some kind of instruction always took place. I count myself lucky to have had amazing mission leaders who taught me valuable life lessons at an early and impressionable age. But I was never specifically taught *yes, and* thinking. I wish I had been. Because I think it's not only one of the most useful skills a missionary can develop, it's native to the gospel of Jesus Christ.

When the Pharisees brought an adulterous woman to Jesus (John 8:5, 7), they said, "Moses in the law commanded us, that such should be

stoned: but what sayest thou?" After ignoring the question, Jesus eventually answered, "He that is without sin among you, let him first cast a stone at her." This is a *yes, and* answer. Because He is essentially saying, *"Yes,* you're correct. According to the Law of Moses, she should be stoned. *And* he that is without sin among you, let him first cast a stone at her."

We see *yes, and* throughout the scriptures, particularly when there's the potential for conflict. In the parable of the Laborers and the Vineyard (Matthew 20:1–16), when all the laborers receive their expected penny, those who had labored since early morning complain that those who were hired at the eleventh hour received equal pay. The goodman of the house tells them, "Yes, you received the payment I promised. And they did, too." An even deeper reading might show his response as, "Yes, you all received your reward, and you are all equal in my eyes."

In the Prodigal Son (Luke 15:11–32), when the father celebrates the return of the younger son, the older brother is so resentful of his father's jubilation that he refuses to participate in the celebratory feast. Note the *yes, and* structure of his father's response. "[Yes] Son, thou art ever with me, and all that I have is thine. [And] It was meet that we should make merry, and be glad: for this

*David Habben*

thy brother was dead, and is alive again; and was lost, and is found."

How might the dialogue have gone between Ammon and King Lamoni (Alma 18) if Ammon had thrown up an unnecessary roadblock by attempting to correct the king's understanding of the Great Spirit?

**26** And then Ammon said: Believest thou that there is a Great Spirit?

**27** And he said, Yea.

**28** And Ammon said: Well, your faith and traditions are all wrong, because God's not actually a spirit. But I'm here to tell you the right way to think about God.

Ammon's actual response is *yes, and* because he discusses with Lamoni, that yes, the Great Spirit is God. And he created all things which are in heaven and in the earth.

One of the most potent scriptural examples of *yes, and* diffusing a tense situation is in Pahoran's response to Moroni's indignant epistle (Alma 61). Much has been made in Sunday School

> **Building relationships of trust is not simply nodding our heads. It's listening. Then affirming. Then contributing.**

and seminary lessons of Pahoran's humility and patience. I think we can also see elements of *yes, and* in his reply. Throughout his epistle he validates Moroni's grievances (the yeses). He also builds on the conversation by giving him news that puts those grievances in context (the ands). His message might be best encapsulated by verse 9: "[Yes] in your epistle you have censured me . . . [and] I am not angry, but do rejoice in the greatness of your heart."

One of the reasons *yes, and* is so compatible with the gospel is because it is so incompatible with an "us versus them" mentality. *Yes, and* is about collaboration, not confrontation. And who in this faith faces potential conflict on a daily basis more than our full-time missionaries?

During my time as a missionary in Eastern Europe, elders often visited a woman who had been a member of the Church for about a year. During one visit, she openly lamented the loss of her Catholic traditions. For decades she'd attended mass, taken communion, lit candles, and gone to confession, all surreptitiously and in defiance of an oppressive Soviet regime. Now, a baptized and confirmed member of a faith new to her and her country, she was missing the familiar and comfortable genuflection, the sign of the cross, rosary beads, and the aroma of incense.

To my shame, while she was sharing her grief, I rolled my eyes in exasperation. She called me out for it and said other elders had responded similarly. I wasn't the first to lose her trust when I told her she should just embrace the restored gospel and not worry about her old traditions. I saw her faith traditions as something to confront, not collaborate with.

I was an inexperienced twenty-year-old whose prefrontal cortex was still in its final stages of development. But what if as part of the training I'd received, I'd been instructed in *yes, and* exchanges? What might have happened if I'd had the insight to say, "Yes, there is great beauty in those ceremonies and rites. And here is how we see ritual and ceremony in the Restored Church . . . " Or "Yes, traditions are important. And, I'd love to know how they bring you closer to Christ." Or "Yes, I understand your Catholic upbringing is dear to you. And, have you noticed similar themes in the Book of Mormon?" There is no end to *and*. That's what makes improv so captivating. It might not have resolved her concerns. But it would have kept the conversation going. And it would have been another step towards Christ for both of us.

President Gordon B. Hinckley often extended this invitation to members of other faiths: "Bring with you all that you have of good and truth which you have received from whatever source, and come and let us see if we may add to it."[3] This is a *yes, and* statement. He was affirming and adding, saying, "*Yes,* you have truth in your faith traditions. *And* we invite you to discover more with us."

A few years ago, I was out with the missionaries assigned to our ward. We went to a house where they said they'd been invited to drop by. Whether it was a mistaken address or a bait-and-switch contact, the owners of the house did not let us in, but immediately launched into an evangelical rant against the Church. They accused the missionaries of spreading un-Christian doctrine and backed up their accusations by citing the first verses of John from memory: "In the beginning was the Word, and the Word was with God, and the Word was God. The same was in the beginning with God. All things were made by him; and without him was not anything made that was made."

They paused, giving the missionaries a chance to respond. Still reeling, one of these stunned elders simply stammered, "But . . . we're here to share the Book of Mormon."

Now, I was as shell-shocked by our reception as these elders were. I was no help at all. But what a missed opportunity. We might have said, "Amen! Praise God! He is the Word!" Despite the hostility, these people offered something we were in complete agreement with. There was no reason to follow that beautiful scripture with "but . . ."

If we're not listening, if we're too eager to say what we want to say, *yes, and* doesn't work. Amy Poehler says when you change the script to stick with your own agenda, "it shows someone's not listening. They don't go along with your initiation. They, in the moment, want to correct you. And also you can't trust them." Building relationships of trust is not simply nodding our heads. It's listening. Then affirming. Then contributing. We never take any of those steps if we confuse conversations with sermons.

In *Yes, And: Lessons from the Second City*, authors Kelly Leonard and Tom Yorton assert that practicing improvisational skills "improves emotional intelligence, teaches you to pivot out of tight and uncomfortable spaces, and helps you become both a more compelling leader and a more collaborative follower." We could all use those skills. But the need for each of them is intensified with the rigors and challenges of full-time mission service. Leonard and Yorton also say, "Work cultures that embrace Yes, And are more inventive, quicker to solve problems, and more likely to have engaged employees than organizations where ideas are judged, criticized, and rejected too quickly." If I were a mission leader, this is exactly the kind of culture I'd want to nurture in the mission. And I'd use *yes, and* training to help us get there.

I haven't been a full-time missionary for decades. But I still have faith-based and faith-laced conversations all the time. And *yes, and* thinking is the most productive and warmhearted approach I've found for discussing religion, no matter who I'm speaking with. I recently went to lunch with a friend and coworker. When our meals arrived, he said he'd like to ask a blessing on the food before we ate. Of course I said, "Yes." And after his prayer, I was conscious of following up with several *ands*. I asked him how he feels God's love in his life. I asked what miracles he sees. I asked his favorite scripture. I didn't have to use the conjunction *and*. But together we were furthering the conversation, when we could have just as easily changed the subject.

Even with someone whose beliefs are antagonistic to mine, I can find a way of saying, "Yes, I think I can understand where you're coming from." That's a major connection, whereas "No, you're totally wrong" simply throws up a wall, leaving me on one side, and them on the other. Us versus them is a barrier we construct ourselves.

Sometimes those barriers we erect are against ourselves. When I was a bishop, members would often come to me with what they perceived as worthiness issues. In these cases, it would have been profoundly detrimental for me to say, "Well, you shouldn't take the sacrament because you're not worthy." *Yes, and* helped me stay intensely set on validating and moving the conversation forward. I might have said any of the following:

"Yes, you've done something you wish you hadn't, and the Savior says over and over throughout the scriptures His hand is stretched out still."

Or "Yes, you're feeling low right now, and in D&C 58:42–43 the Lord says He is willing to forget this completely."

Or "Yes, that's a serious issue, and you're amazingly brave to be open to talking about it."

Or "Yes, I see why you feel you're not worthy to take the sacrament now, and did you know the General Handbook says, 'Partaking of the sacrament is an important part of repentance. It should not be the first restriction given to a repentant person who has a broken heart and contrite spirit'?"

Again, there is no end to *and*.

*Yes, and* is the golden rule of improv. But it is also the hidden subtext to our most Christlike interactions. We are all collaborators on this mortal stage. If we're willing to listen to our fellow actors, hear their prompts, repress our personal agendas, and respond with *yes, and*, we can all move the scene forward together. ✳

1.   Kelly Leonard and Tom Yorton, "Yes, And: How to Make Something Out of Nothing," in *Yes, And: How Improvisation Reverses "No, But" Thinking and Improves Creativity and Collaboration* (New York: HarperCollins, 2015), 3–4, 13.

2.   "Prepare to Be Unprepared with Amy Poehler," Master-Class, 2023.

3.   Gordon B. Hinckley, "The Marvelous Foundation of Our Faith," *Ensign*, November 2002, 78–81.

# JAREDITES ON THE WAVES OF THE GREAT DEEP

MEGAN
McMANAMA

*Ether 2:24 For behold, ye shall be as a whale in the midst of the sea; for the mountain waves shall dash upon you. Nevertheless, I will bring you up again out of the depths of the sea; for the winds have gone forth out of my mouth, and also the rains and the floods have I sent forth.*

I dream in waves, I wake
in waves, I speak in waves. I cannot help
but murmur. Yesterday we were rising up
a watery mountain, today we are swallowed down
to its belly: a tomb at the bottom of everything.

But always, you
lift us up again.

I find solace in two things:
      these rocks, like parents,
taken up the Mount, past the veil,
and touched by the King of Kings himself.
In this vessel, they hold me at night,
caress my back in thunder, and whisper
my name gently. They're as bright
as two little suns.

      And how at times, we remove the opening,
take back the pavilion and let the holy air
slip in like bird song in the morning.
Not just air, but sometimes dappled sun
and starlight pillar down, we watch
it like a firelight dancing at our feet.
It is our only art, only hope, a song of some
holy just outside.
For a moment the waves feel
familiar. As if mother holds her hand
to her belly, how she lulls us, how she rocks us,
as she walks home.

# THEN SHALL THEY FAST

DAVID L.
TAYMAN III

YEARS AGO, A LOVED ONE DIED, AND I was led to wonder if it might have been my fault.

I had unintentionally left my phone on silent for several hours and discovered that during this time it had amassed an atypical number of missed calls. The first voicemail gave the reason for the urgent volume: a family member had suffered a sudden and severe medical emergency, and I was being desperately contacted in hope that my prayer could be added to those already pleading for divine healing. In what was hours for those experiencing the crisis, but a matter of seconds for me, I reached the last message; the urgency in the voice of the caller had been replaced with resignation and devastation. It was too late. The person had died.

Would it have made a difference if I had been able to join the prayer vigil, and add my voice to the tally of concerned believers in Christ pleading for that life to be saved?

If I truly believed that "the prayer of the righteous is powerful and effective" (James 5:16), then shouldn't I be required to acknowledge that my prayer could have tipped the scales? If I thought my inability to be present to add my petition among those of others wouldn't have changed the outcome, would that mean I was rejecting a belief in truly efficacious prayer? Did absentmindedly leaving my phone on silent cause the intercessory tally to just not quite add up to what God needed it to be? Was it my fault he died?

I didn't believe that then, and I don't believe it now. But I have found myself in the position to be directly challenged about that perspective. And being able to clearly articulate the 'whys' and 'hows' of the conviction of my position beyond simply an expression of feeling that it just can't work that way has been a surprisingly elusive endeavor.

Reflecting on this experience alone wasn't quite enough to provide me with a definitive, comprehensive solution to the complex age-old question of the relationship between human and divine agency.

But a side effect was that it did complicate my relationship with fasting. That ended up being a hidden blessing, as it was in working through the problem using this lens that I was guided toward a framework that would enable me to better articulate "the hope that is in [me]" (1 Peter 3:15) regarding the power and utility of prayer.

I grew up in a Christian tradition where fasting was on the margins of my early religious life. But as a mature adult Latter-day Saint convert, I could no longer avoid thinking about and practicing fasting, which now entered as a regularly scheduled part of my religious routine.

The discipline of fasting forms part of the inheritance of countless spiritual traditions around the world. The value found in the practice, the reasons for it, and the meanings attached to it can be even more varied than the methods and rules by which it is accomplished.

There are many aspects of the particular Latter-day Saint approach to fasting that resonated with me from the beginning of my exposure to it, and that remains true. I loved the practice of transferring the cost of meals given up into contributions to those in need. I understood how the voluntarily induced pangs of hunger could turn one's heart empathetically to those who experienced those pains involuntarily and far more sharply. I appreciated the discipline of consciously denying one's physical needs to focus on the nourishing of the spiritual. I saw value in the scheduled monthly observance and integration of it into our public worship cycle. All of those things made sense and were effective devotional practices that turned my thoughts to the life of Christ, as I believe all devotional practices should. And they made scriptures such as Isaiah's discussion about proper fasts, and the gospel accounts

of Jesus's fasting in the wilderness come alive, with immediate and personal application.

But what I never fully understood was the practice of *fasting for an intended miraculous result*. I had experienced enough cases in my own personal life where fasting occurred in the face of impending tragedy and ongoing painful degenerative illness, and yet as far as I could recognize, no cure or balm in Gilead arose. No miraculous change of the situation parted the waters. No transformation of hearts to accept peacefully and piously that God must have wanted or needed that loved one to suffer. In those cases, I wondered if the fasting was wasted. In the cases where others in the family or congregation joined in, did a community of people just go hungry for a few hours without benefit (with the exception of those who were fed by the suggested accompanying offering)?

What was the point? This train of thought led to additional questions. In the cases where fasting *did* result in a seeming miraculous outcome, could that not have occurred without the fasting? Or was the communal act indeed the key that unlocked a window in the heavens otherwise jammed shut? I knew the traditional scriptural passage where Jesus "said unto them, 'This kind can come forth by nothing, but by prayer and fasting'" (Mark 9:29 KJV), but what did it mean? (And it was further complicated by the knowledge that the addition of 'fasting' to 'prayer' is understood by many scholars as a later addition to the text.)

Despite my questions, I'd still participate in fasts for causes, asking for the deeply desired blessing with sincere faith that God could provide, but sadly low on hope that the physical self-denying action itself was actually moving the needle in any substantial way.

Could one extra person giving up a meal make the difference between life and death? Could a missed phone call make the difference? Did questioning this make my fast a "dead work"?

With these ideas always somewhere in the margins of my thoughts, it was in the course of my regular study of the New Testament that a passage I'd read many times before, but had never thought much about, gave me pause.

## Could one extra person giving up a meal make the difference between life and death? Did questioning this make my fast a "dead work"?

In the fifth chapter of Luke, Jesus and his small crew of new disciples are being challenged for their lack of communal participation in the act of fasting—something we had just been shown Jesus personally doing on his own one chapter earlier.

"They said to him, 'John's disciples, like the disciples of the Pharisees, frequently fast and pray, but your disciples eat and drink.' Jesus said to them, 'You cannot make wedding attendants fast while the bridegroom is with them, can you? The days will come when the bridegroom will be taken away from them, and then they will fast in those days'" (Luke 5:33–35 NRSV:UE).

The imagery of Christ as the Bridegroom and the Church as the Bride (and somewhat paradoxically also the wedding guests) was very familiar to me, as was the picture of the Banquet in the Kingdom of Heaven in the Age to Come. But I had never associated the scene with the practice of fasting, as was done here. There are many scriptures regularly used to promote the practice of fasting,[1] but this one doesn't usually come up, likely because on its surface, it's giving a reason why Jesus and his disciples were actively *not* fasting.

Looking into that space, though, provided an answer for me.

When were they not fasting? *When the Bridegroom/Savior was with them.*

When would they fast again? *When Jesus had left their presence, and they were anticipating his return*, essentially a reset of the story.

This observation changed my perspective to consider that when we're preparing to dine with Christ in his Kingdom, a fast is actively protecting our appetites for when he arrives, when we will feast in full; that is when the fast will end, the object or intention of the fast having been accomplished. It's been suggested that when Christ fed the multitudes with the miraculous loaves and fishes, he was giving them a sample of

> ## As we regularly ask for those morsels of daily bread, through fasting we are acknowledging with our full body *that the full banquet hasn't arrived yet.*

that eschatological banquet. He was giving them their "daily bread" in a preview of the ultimate Messianic Meal.[2]

Can we similarly put ourselves in this mindset when we participate in the sacrament of the Lord's Supper? We are feasting together in memory of when Christ last feasted with his Apostles, and in anticipation of feasting once again in the presence of Christ.[3]

When we fast, we can recall that we're in the period following the last supper. "Then they will fast," Jesus said. They did, and so do we.

While the ultimate hope is centered on the coming of Christ, it is tied up in everything the arrival of the Kingdom of God in its fullness would signal. The passage from Isaiah Jesus read in the synagogue in Chapter 4 of Luke is what Jesus's disciples were actively experiencing then, and what we are tempering our appetite for as we fast:

> Good news to the poor. Release to the captives. Recovery of sight to the blind. The setting free of those who are oppressed. The proclamation of the year of the Lord's favor.

What if that's the ultimate object of our fast? As we regularly ask for those morsels of daily bread, through fasting we are acknowledging with our full body that the full banquet hasn't arrived yet and won't until we are again with Christ. And when we have short-term fulfillments of those objectives in place, we may be seeking them out

of a desire and wish to have a very specific portion of that "daily bread" today, but with an expression of hope that the full meal will come regardless. We aren't demanding an early snack in place of the banquet, but we certainly won't reject it if by the grace of God it is given.

It's common practice to end a Latter-day Saint fast with a prayer, where the object of the fast is again considered and requested. What comes next is often a full Sunday dinner. Sometimes it's just a sandwich, or a handful of chips. But no matter the food, it tastes great. It fills the hunger. Sometimes you go a little too fast and overindulge. But you feast.

When I fast, I still want the "now" answer to my prayer. I want the cancer cured. I want the infertility to be resolved. I want chronic pain removed. I want death to be staved off, and those who have died to return to be with me.[4]

And if any of those things happen today or tomorrow, I will give thanks for that grace and confess the hand of the Lord.

But if not, I no longer have any reason to consider my fast a dead work. I see it now as

> ## I'm making myself vulnerable, voluntarily walking into the wilderness, hungry, waiting for the blessings of the fulness of Christ's Kingdom to arrive in my life in whatever way they come.

a powerful physical way to manifest the dual Christian imperatives to mourn with those who mourn (Mosiah 18:9), and express steadfast assurance that the blessed hope is coming (Hebrews 6:18–19). I'm making myself vulnerable, voluntarily walking into the wilderness,[5] hungry, waiting for the blessings of the fulness of Christ's Kingdom to arrive in my life in whatever way they come.

I'm expressing hope that in due time, after a period of frustration and pain, after we "cry

*Rose Datoc Dall*

for help . . . he will say, 'Here I am'" (Isaiah 58:9 NRSV:UE), and we will all feast together as complete, joyful persons in the presence of the Bridegroom. I can experience the peace of renewed hope now, even as I mourn.[6] Indeed, though it was obscured from me for so long, I now see clearly this passage from the Doctrine and Covenants: "Verily, this is fasting and prayer, or in other words, rejoicing and prayer" (Doctrine & Covenants 59:14). ✳

1.   For example, Isaiah 58, especially verses 6–7.

2.   Consider that it is directly following the introduction of the Lord's Prayer with this petition for "daily bread" that Jesus gives instructions about *"when* ye fast" (Matthew 6:16–18; 3 Nephi 13:16–18).

3.   For example: "Jesus' symbolic praxis of feasting with his followers, and of weaving stories around this prac-tice . . . [is] regularly, and rightly, seen as a symbolic evocation of the coming messianic banquet. . . . Jesus' feastings, and the stories he told which reflect this practice, are to be read in this context, as are, per-haps, the accounts of extraordinary feedings of large crowds." N. T. Wright, *Jesus and the Victory of God* (Minneapolis: Fortress Press, 1996), 532.

4.   See Alma 28:4–6: "And now this was a time that there was a great mourning and lamentation. . . . Yea, the cry of widows mourning for their husbands, and also of fathers mourning for their sons, and the daughter for the brother, yea, the brother for the father; and thus the cry of mourning was heard among all of them, mourning for their kindred who had been slain. And now surely this was a sorrowful day; yea, a time of so-lemnity, and a time of much fasting and prayer."

5.   See Matthew 4:1–2: "Then Jesus was led up by the Spirit into the wilderness. . . . He fasted forty days and forty nights, and afterward he was famished."

6.   As Jesus wept with his friends who were mourning Lazarus's death even in the moments before restoring him to them. See John 11:35.

# THE ATONEMENT OF LOVE

*Presence, Suffering, Transformation*

**SAMUEL BROWN**

AS AN EXCEEDINGLY EARNEST missionary in the early 1990s, I found myself transfixed by one prominent story about the Atonement. It had to do with the way that our individual sins affected Christ's suffering. I knew then with perfect clarity that every time I committed a minor deviation from the White Bible (the then-current missionary handbook, a pocket-sized rule book binding missionaries across the church), I was pounding a nail into Christ's battered flesh on the cross at Golgotha. With each tiny sin—staying sixty-one minutes at a dinner, say—I was directly responsible for a new portion of Christ's terrible punishment. This image played a part in a scrupulousness that made me impossible to live with as a missionary. I tried to skip Preparation Day so that I could keep proselytizing; I never told (or laughed at) jokes; I memorized huge swaths of scripture. I could not escape the feeling that my mortal inadequacy brutalized the suffering Christ.

That searing image motivated me to magnificent productivity as a young missionary: no one worked harder than I did. And now I wonder. I find myself asking lately: is that actually how the Atonement works? Why, in the final account, did Christ suffer in the Garden and on the Hill? In what sense might I and my sins have been present with him in one or both of those places? As I navigate life's middle places, I find that the answers to these questions that resonate with me now are different from those that resonated with the young Elder Brown. I'm not looking for permission to be religiously less committed; nor am I bothered by the possibility that external standards might in fact apply to me. I just keep staring at Atonement and wondering what all it contains.

Atonement is one of the most basic problems to vex Christians over the millennia. I think that because it is both so basic and so vast, Atonement leaves most of us befuddled. The cruel death of Jesus Christ is certainly one of the stranger twists in history and theology, and many believe that this vulnerability of a God stands at the center of the Christian revolution. No one but the Christians, it seems, was eager to worship a God so fragile, so weak, so vulnerable. Wikipedia, that electric menagerie of the stupid and the useful, counts approximately nine distinct theories of Atonement. More sophisticated treatments than Wikipedia may favor greater or lesser numbers of Atonement theories depending on their

**Penal substitution mostly maintains that we mortals have a just and overwhelming punishment awaiting us because we have broken a law. But our hopelessness is remedied by an unusual feature of this law: a willing substitute can bear the penalty in our place. That's what makes a savior.**

theological emphasis and whether they like their categories big or small. In our Restoration tradition, for example, the philosopher-attorney Blake Ostler has carefully summarized four Latter-day Saint theories of Atonement. Something as earth-shattering and paradigm-breaking as Atonement is going to generate much wonder, confusion, and wobbly words.

Some ancient authors saw Christ as a "ransom" paid to liberate us from captivity to Satan. Other thinkers saw Christ's death as meeting the mandates of something like a law that we humans had broken, a vicarious punishment. Others saw Atonement as a graciously persuasive act, with Christ demonstrating a willingness to give of himself that we should emulate. The late English professor and peacemaking activist Gene England promoted within Latter-day Saint thought this "moral suasion" model of Atonement ultimately attributed to the medieval theologian Peter Abelard. There are many possible paths to the reconciliation of God and humanity; these theories of Atonement point out several of those paths.

My best guess is that we Latter-day Saints favor substitutionary or penal understandings of Atonement. That's the one I heard most often in the late twentieth century, more often than not tied up in a theory that sounded more Star Wars than Scripture, in which every molecule in the universe actively demanded that justice be served. I don't hear that theory—the anti-Communist

Cleon Skousen's strange adaptation of Orson Pratt's panpsychism—much anymore, but I still remember that image of atoms clamoring for blood at a galactic tribunal. Stripped of Skousen's filigree, though, penal substitution mostly maintains that we mortals have a just and overwhelming punishment awaiting us because we have broken a law. But our hopelessness is remedied by an unusual feature of this law: a willing substitute can bear the penalty in our place. That's what makes a savior. On this account, Christ acted something like the distraught father who confesses to a crime in order to take his son's place on the gallows.

This approach to Atonement may sound strange to a late-modern ear—all this talk about punishment and sin and violated cosmic order doesn't sound the same as it once did. We late-moderns are often deeply unsympathetic to the underlying worlds in which this theory made deep and satisfying sense. And I'm not arguing that we should abandon it. The penal substitution model still has much to recommend it. There is a sense in which right is in fact right and our distance from rightness needs to be healed. No matter how much we late-modern folk squirm about external standards, in our hearts I think most of us still sense that we could be better than we are. And we feel painful shame and longing when we acknowledge the moral distance between who we are and who we might be. Penal substitution takes these facts square on and proposes a solution.

We should acknowledge, too, the emotional heft of the penal substitution theory. The image of Christ taking lashes for us is a sacred and moving one. My heart breaks at the thought of a soul-deep love that could motivate Christ to sacrifice health and happiness for me. I'm not as ready as many another modern believer to abandon the penal understanding of Atonement, and I'll never be ready to accuse those who believe it of heartlessness. It is not cruel to yearn for a world of order and meaning that may call us to be better than we would otherwise be. We don't have to imagine that God is cruel to believe that God may need to transform us, and that transformation may be difficult, even painful, for all involved. The theology is deep here, deeper than any easy answers.

But still, I wonder. What if this idea of penal substitution doesn't capture the vastness of Christ's sacrifice? What if our vision has been blurred by conflicting modern concepts of bureaucratic uniformity, personal identity, and individualism? What if there is another form and aspect of *relation* at play in Atonement? The longer I've spent wrestling with these topics, the more convinced I am that we as Latter-day Saints have access to a more profound sense of identity-in-community than we have generally confessed. And that more basic principle may hold the key to a broader understanding of Atonement as the transformative identity of humans and Gods.

Latter-day Saint theologians have made important progress in this century toward a Restoration theology of Atonement. Blake Ostler sketched out a mixed theory of Atonement he called Compassionate in the middle aughts. Ostler emphasized sin as alienation from God, our goal in life as movement toward sanctification/deification in Christ's light, and Christ's unique ability to call us into lived union on the basis of his compassion. This divine-human compassion is born of Christ's experience of the full range of human suffering. The feminist philosopher and Kierkegaard scholar Deidre Green argued that Ostler was still too indebted to penal models. Green focused especially on the hypothetical risk that for Ostler repentance transferred suffering to Christ and might thereby induce believers—especially women who may be more prone to self-sacrifice—to refuse to repent in the interests of saving Christ the pain of their repented sin. (My younger self would probably have agreed with them.) Green's criticism led Ostler to a cleaner and more persuasive elaboration of his Compassion theory of Atonement.[1] Admitting inevitable differences, Ostler's account overlapped some with an account by the engineer-blogger Jacob Morgan, who saw the light of Christ as an "infusion" which transformed and saved believers. I am grateful for these recent accounts focused on the experience of compassion and the brass tacks of shared life among mortal and divine souls. They are helpful antecedents to what I see as an Atonement of Love.

As I see it, Atonement is intimately tied to the miracle of Incarnation, what the Book of Mormon calls Christ's condescension. Christ, being divine, became human. He condescended to join us in mortality. Incarnation and condescension aren't identical terms, but they're quite close: Atonement is about humans becoming divine, while Incarnation is about the divine becoming human. The two meet in Christ.

Note that Incarnation already marks Christ as mortal, with critical ramifications. Joining us in mortality means that Christ becomes vulnerable to mortality's indignities, including illness and death. Why did Jesus have to die? That part seems simple: because he was human. Being born means having to die. That's what *mortal* means. But by the time Christ gave up the ghost as an

*J. Kirk Richards*

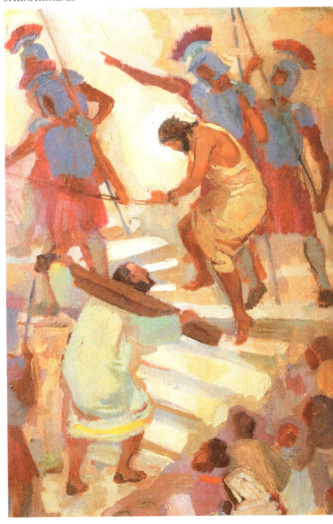

adult, that work was already done. He'd been mortal for decades.

I have just begged a critical question: In saying that Christ died because he was human, I didn't ask why he became human in the first place. My best guess is that he became human because Divinity has to enter the world somehow. Otherwise we are left godless, just bits of matter that pass through some imagined awareness and then disappear back into the entropic mist that will one day culminate in the heat death of the universe. Without the entry of Divinity into the world, we are just stardust that thinks it can think and pretends it can matter. But how does the chasm between the thinly material world of people and the glorious realm of Divinity get bridged? That's what Atonement is concerned with. The problem of Incarnation is fundamentally a question about whether divine

*J. Kirk Richards*

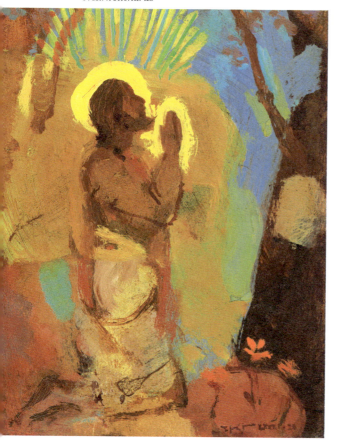

## Without the entry of Divinity into the world, we are just stardust that think it can think and pretends it can matter.

transcendence (perhaps as spiritually fine matter; perhaps as more than that) can enter our coarse and fallen world. That seems straightforward enough, even traditional, as an answer. And it strikes me as probably true. Christ is the affirmative answer to the question: can God be present with us in this world? That divine presence, that *Immanuel*, is Christ's human life.

But we still haven't gotten to the question of Christ's suffering as we Latter-day Saints understand it. Why did the passionate misery of Gethsemane have to happen if the entry of Christ into earth life was *already* a reconciliation of the Divine and the human? Why couldn't Christ have died as a newborn, touching his toes to earth just long enough to transform the world but not long enough to suffer? Why couldn't Christ have died in his sleep?

Here I believe we witness the sacred extension of Incarnation to Atonement, encompassing not just mortality as the susceptibility to death but identity with us across the range of our human experience. Not only did Christ need to become flesh—in some sense, he needed to become *us*. What if, in other words, the suffering in Gethsemane was Christ opening himself to all of us at a metaphysical and ontological level? And not just to all of us in the sense of every human who ever lives (every *one* of us), but all of us in the sense of the full extremity of each one of us (every *part* of us). In those depths stand much pain, selfishness, sin, grief, and tragedy. We know that, instinctively. We are difficult to love. Indeed, it is painful. And yet Christ did just that, and in that encounter between perfect love and twisted mortality, I believe, comes the intense pain of the Garden of Gethsemane. In this respect I find that I generally agree with Ostler and Green that what is luminously true in Atonement is this fact of identity and union. I suspect that I am more skeptical of late-modern ideas about selfhood than they are, but on this basic principle, I think we agree in a fundamentally Latter-day Saint way.

In this understanding of Atonement, it remains true that Christ took upon himself our sins, our churlish buffoonery, our impatience, stupidity, cupidity, and cruelty. That's all true. But maybe he didn't do it just to meet the demands of a cosmic criminal justice system. I'm sure that whatever law might be operative was in fact satisfied with Christ's sacrifice. But I don't think that's the whole story. Maybe, at a fundamental level, Christ took upon himself our sins because *that's what it means to love us.* We are, unavoidably, painful to love. We are the infants who shriek through the night no matter how tenderly the parents try to soothe. We are the children who kick and steal and curse. We are the partners who betray, belittle, and violate. We are the narcissistic exhibitionists who can hear no voice but their own. And there God stands, through Jesus, loving us anyway. Loving every hard and painful bit of us. No matter how much it hurts God to do so. This is not the vacuous love that is indifferent to the shape of our lives as some pop psychologists might have it. God's love will transform us: that is, after all, the end game for the Atonement. That transformation will be painful, and it is the best thing that could ever happen to us.

I respect the ideaworld underlying the penal model of Atonement, even if specific instances of it may miss the point. We really won't be godly If our whole lives are spent choosing against God. If we've never tried in life, it's strange in the extreme to imagine that we will be wholly godly right after life draws to a close. But the penal model of Atonement is just that, a model. It's not the same to walk across a map of Paris in your basement as it is to wander along the River Seine. Nor is it the same to imagine a terribly just God (or Eternal Law) extracting punishment as it is to experience Atonement itself.

When we actually experience Atonement, we realize, I think, why it was that Christ had to suffer. Because the pure love of a mortal being is inextricable from suffering. To put it too simply, it hurts to love us. This is not meant to demean us humans, but rather to glorify us. However painful

> When we actually experience Atonement, we realize, I think, why it was that Christ had to suffer. Because the pure love of a mortal being is inextricable from suffering. To put it too simply, it hurts to love us.

we are to love, Christ and our heavenly parents love us anyway. In their love, we have life.

In this realization comes another view on that haunting tableau with which we began. I was a missionary convinced that I was a Roman soldier, spear stabbing into Christ's side, every time I missed five minutes of study time or smiled at a woman my age. It's not that I, inveterate sinner that I was and am, was actively killing Christ. I never have and never will send a spike through his wrist. When we sin, we are causing our own suffering. And Christ in his infinite love that fully infiltrates our identity has agreed that he will always love us no matter how painful it might be. The worse we are as people, the more noxious it is to love us, true. But Christ won't stop loving us, no matter what. The heavenly parents don't love us as the easy path; they don't love us for some benefit to themselves, some flames of parental pride they must stoke with the kindling of our broken lives. Their love for us is a grace beyond any such calculations of risk and benefit. Theirs is an Atonement of Love, of being in relation, of identity.

One strength of this relational theory of Atonement is that it's true to our mortal experience. We have all at some point felt what it is to love another imperfect being. There is great beauty and power in such love, and there is sadness. Sometimes such terrible sadness. Even if the beloved is nearly perfect, there is still the exquisite and soul-searing reality that all beloveds will one day die. To love well is to experience pain. I have known the soul-deep terror of loving a person who is struck by terrible illness and then dies. That love, however painful, is nothing I would ever walk away from.

Among the most sacred memories of my late adolescence was the discovery of how many people had prayed and wept on my behalf as I made a string of bad decisions and cultivated a life estranged from God and sanctity. We know, if we are honest, that we have caused pain to those mortals who love us. And we know how sacred it is to be loved through our failings. If Christ truly loves us, then, why would he be free from that pain? In other words, why would Gethsemane not have been painful? *No reason at all.*

What I'm suggesting here is that the horrible pain in Gethsemane might have been the moment when Christ was allowed to love us all, perfectly. Until then, perhaps, he had not reached the necessary phase of his earthly development. For reasons I confess are not immediately apparent to me, his Incarnation had not yet become our incarnation. We were not yet fully his in the Atoning work of adoption. And as we became his, as our stubborn identities melted into Christ's cosmos-ordering love, we became one with Christ and with our heavenly parents.

This Atonement of Love reinterprets many traditional texts. Take Doctrine & Covenants 18—Christ "suffereth the pains of all men." Or consider the deeply Christological texts in Isaiah—"he hath borne our griefs and carried our sorrows." Or the account of 2 Nephi, "he suffereth the pains of all men, yea, the pains of every living creature, both men, women, and children, who belong to the family of Adam." I'm aware that a bewildered if metaphysically potent scapegoat, bearing the sins of the community, may lurk just offstage in certain scriptural passages. What I'm arguing is that Christ gives us license to read these rituals and their textual echoes as pointing beyond themselves to larger truths about the nature of love.

Amulek's influential references in Alma 34 to "an infinite and eternal sacrifice" which functions as an "infinite atonement" also resonate differently within an Atonement of Love. Amulek explains that you can't kill a murderer's brother to resolve the murderer's guilt. Culpability and punishment don't naturally, logically, or legally transfer from one person to another. Instead there

will be an infinite end to sacrifice that "encircles [sinners] in the arms of safety." Admitting that the Amulek text touches on multiple theories of Atonement simultaneously, I see in that infinite Atonement a kind of red thread of fate tying Christ and us together, forever.

This concept of a relational Atonement of Love has an array of implications. It provides different context for old stories in ways that are true to the old and open to the new.

For example, acknowledging how painful it is to love mortals makes some sense of our teaching that God and the cosmos suffered terribly when Christ died. As he breathed his last, earthquakes raked the New World, and the temple's veil in the Old World split in two, as if the temple were tearing its garment in grief. Our heavenly parents wept just as they did when they watched with Enoch over the full expanse of human history. As Enoch sees all of humanity, he and "the God of heaven" stand together, their faces wet with sadness, witnessing the human penchant for wickedness and cruelty. A mystified Enoch asks God why God is crying. God replies, in essence, that it hurts to love us. But he loves us anyway. (While the scripture, true to its time, doesn't mention her, in my mind's eye, I have often seen the Heavenly Mother crying with Enoch and the Father in that stark and beautiful panorama of human history that prefigures the Garden of Gethsemane.)

Within the Atonement of Love, Christ can judge us because he *is* us. Who better to judge us than the one who has merged his Divine identity with our mortal identity? Who has loved every nook and cranny of us, no matter how blighted or cruel or pathetic? I've long thought that the best way to understand the familiar and too-often-cruel maxim "Love the Sinner; Hate the Sin" is to perform a thought experiment: imagine that you are the sinner. In other words, think about how you would feel if you were the one who had committed the sin. Not some stranger, some spiteful enemy. You. How heavy would you want the punishment to be, and how would you feel about the fact of punishment? In general, we would want only the absolute minimum of punishment necessary to the task, and we would feel no hatred for

J. Kirk Richards

**Within the Atonement of Love, Christ can judge us because he *is* us. Who better to judge us than the one who has merged his Divine identity with our mortal identity? Who has loved every nook and cranny of us, no matter how blighted or cruel or pathetic?**

the offender. You may still need to send a person to prison for certain crimes. But you should ache at the thought of it, mourn the fact of the pain and punishment, and seek to make the punishment as tolerable as possible. Because that's what we would do for ourselves. That seems to me what Christ does in judgment. He joins with us in perfect communion and is able to imagine the world from our perspective, deeply and painfully in love with us. Judgment without communion is just alienation. Judgment in communion is precisely what this relational model of the Atonement of Love is. When we truly and rapturously love the sinner, we participate directly in Atonement. And when we hate the sinner, we reject the Atonement. In contempt for the sinner, we refuse Christ's Way.

But we need not refuse love. Christ's Way, Christ's Love, is as universal as stardust, wind, and sunlight. There is liberty in this universal scope of atoning love. While I am no Universalist in the non-Mormon sense, the Atonement of Love sees beyond salvation to the actual saving beauty that animates it. When we fret about whether we're saved, we turn the story of our lives inward, following the modernist script of isolated consumers pleasing and perfecting themselves. With the Atonement of Love, we turn the story of our lives outward. Christ says, "I've got salvation figured out for you. I bathe you in my love. Now I need you to be vessels of my love and grace. So,

you poor broken thing, go shed forth my love in the world." The shift from pious narcissism to Christian agape is the path that the Atonement of Love makes possible.

I know that the Atonement is strange no matter how we conceive it. Especially in our late-modern age—both captivated by and deeply fearful of particularity—we wonder why any specific concrete mechanism might apply. We feel compelled to believe that our own particularity is praiseworthy, even essential. But we dare not attribute such particularity to the cosmos when it interacts with us. That strikes us as too close to constraint, an impingement on our agency. Why wouldn't God just love us enough to save us instead of requiring that such love come through Christ's expansively mortal life? If Atonement is all about Love, in other words, why isn't the Love of God enough? What I'm suggesting is that God and cosmos can be particular too. I think it likely that the Atonement is *how God loves us.* We cannot package God's love into a positive psychology trope or a snippet of poetic Romanticism. We must be open to the possibility that God's love is specific, not just in its capacity to love each of us individually but in the possibility that the shape of that love is at least partly external to us (see, for example, 2 Nephi 2:11). We may need, in other words, to allow for God a majesty that we cannot hold in our hands. For me, that possibility is exhilarating, even as it is terrifying.

This is heady stuff. And anything big and beautiful can miss its mark when we put it to work in human lives. Christ loves us totally, in a way that brings our selves into his. We mortals seek to live that way too, and we see glimmers of it in the astonishing love of a parent for an afflicted child, a friendship that must surely date to the premortal existence, or a wonderfully healthy marriage. But we will also encounter distorted shadows of this pure love. We see this most clearly in an abuser who seeks domination in the name of unity, stamping out the partner's self. Christ does not call the abused to seek identity with the abuser. God forbid. Patterns of abuse are not just evil in their own right, but they are also terrible because they distort the true order of love. We must keep our eyes open to those who suffer, always. And in rejecting the misuse of true principles, we must not also deprive ourselves as a community of flourishing, here and now and forever, through Christ's Atoning love.

The atoning love of Christ calls us into painful and glorious communion. It binds us with the unconditional love of a parent willing to sacrifice all for a suffering child. Recognizing that we are painful to love and that Christ has gladly taken on himself that pain is the best and most potent liberty of all. ✳

1.  Blake T. Ostler, "The Compassion Theory of Atonement," in *Exploring Mormon Thought: The Problems of Theism and the Love of God* (Salt Lake City: Greg Kofford Books, 2006).

*J. Kirk Richards*

# Minerva!

## ARTIST, PIONEER, MOTHER

**MADISON BAKER**

*Deposition*

**SAFET ZEC**

# MOTHER TONGUES

**JOHN ALBA CUTLER**

WE KNEEL TO PRAY, AND AS USUAL, I jostle with my younger brother for the right to rest my head and elbows on the couch. We keep the fighting quiet, or Dad will tell us to knock it off and turn around, and when it's Mom's turn to pray, we need the extra support because we know it will last forever. She prays for everything—for each member of our family by name, for the missionaries, for the prophet, for safety, for the Spirit to guide us to make good choices, and for a hundred other things that I don't really understand, both because I am a child, and because Mom only prays in Spanish.

We live in Centerville, Utah, in an unremarkable brick house. We look like most other families, but with darker skin, especially in the summer when my brothers and I turn brown brown brown. We have Mormonad and U2 posters on our walls, Transformers and Barbies in the toy bins, a basketball hoop in the backyard. But we eat beans and homemade flour tortillas, enchiladas and chile verde, and, on Christmas Eve, tamales at our güelitos' house in Salt Lake City. We have wooden tops and hand-sewn dolls and a picture of Mom dancing folklórico on the wall. I'm the only kid at school, as far as I can tell, that

*Sarah Winegar*

*Sarah Winegar*

has güelitos instead of grandparents, the only one that visits a blue house filled with color and warm smells and laughter of a different pitch and volume than I hear anywhere else. And Mom only prays in Spanish.

Her voice lowers almost to a whisper when she prays, and she always begins the same way. Not *Our Dear Heavenly Father, we thank thee for this day* but *Nuestro Amado Padre Celestial, en este día estamos agradecidos.*

I grow up in an enchanted world. God simply *is*. Everyone I know well belongs to the church. Everyone believes, or at least acts like they believe. Everyone prays. All the time. We pray over meals. We pray at the beginning of meetings. We pray morning and noon and night. But when my mom prays, it is different.

My broken Spanish keeps me from understanding large portions of her prayers, surely one reason they seem to last forever. My oldest sister still speaks and understands Spanish perfectly, but in descending birth order we are less and less fluent. I won't speak Spanish well

until I study and practice as a missionary in Pennsylvania; that's still years away. But it's not just the non-understanding that makes Mom's prayers different. It's the intimacy of her voice when she calls on God, the feeling of comfort and safety it generates.

I am pushing and squirming with my brother, sometimes giggling, and I hear *Nuestro Amado Padre Celestial*, and God feels *beloved*. Or not beloved, a word I wouldn't recognize, but loved and loving. I am warmed by the intimacy of my mother's prayer. Later, I will come to understand these family prayers as my first experiences with the Spirit, which is another way of naming a paradox: my Spanish is broken and halting, but Spanish is also my first language of the gospel, my mother's tongue, and my spiritual mother tongue.

It's important for me to remember my mother's prayers, because I have so often experienced and encountered language as alienation.

As a missionary twenty-five years ago, I served in a small, Spanish-speaking branch in Lancaster, Pennsylvania, the only non-English language unit in the mission at that time. We met in the basement of the chapel, usually no more than twenty people on any given Sunday. Most of the members were Puerto Rican, Cuban, and Dominican, though the first person we taught was a young man from Oaxaca, Mexico. They were line cooks, day laborers, construction workers, house cleaners, and nannies, whereas the adults I knew in the English-speaking ward were lawyers, businessmen, doctors, and stay-at-home mothers (which I recognized as a privilege for the first time in my life). The English-speaking ward provided the branch president and a high councilor, and I had the sense that we were somehow the shadow or younger sibling of the real ward.

Members of the English-speaking ward were always kind, and often invited us to dinner. But they said things that moved around in my mind like a pebble in a shoe. "It's too bad that the branch can't support itself," they'd say. "How can we help them assimilate?"

"If they'd just learn English," they'd say. This last point seemed somehow like the key to everything. "English is the language of the Restoration," one brother told me. It was also the key to acculturation, so maybe learning English would unlock both spiritual and material doors.

The Lancaster branch was also my first experience working with youth who were, like me, *no sabo* kids, though this was long before "*no sabo* kid" was a thing. *No sabo.* I don't know. Except in standard Spanish you say *no sé*. You'd only say *no sabo* if you didn't understand how to conjugate the irregular verb *saber*, to know, so you did it like any other verb. If your language was broken. So you're a *no sabo* kid. Your mom or your dad or your grandparents or all-of-the-above talk to you in Spanish, but you answer back in English. Or, in the case of the youth I worked with in Lancaster, then later when I lived in stakes in Los Angeles and Chicago, and now Oakland, you are surrounded not only by family members who speak to you in Spanish,

## Members of the English-speaking ward were always kind, and often invited us to dinner. But they said things that moved around in my mind like a pebble in a shoe. "It's too bad that the branch can't support itself," they'd say. "How can we help them assimilate?"

but also youth leaders who view church as an opportunity for you to practice and perfect your language skills. Suddenly, your mother tongue becomes a chore and a site of judgment.

It's alienation all the way down. *Alienation*, derived from the Latin word *alienare*, or "to estrange." We encounter one another as strangers, or we are estranged from one another, even despite familial or community or ecclesiastical relationships meant to draw us together. There is no more estranging experience than not being able to communicate. You are trying to ask your güelita: "What was your dad like?" and all that comes out is, "*y tu papá . . .*" and then the long silence until your mom intervenes. And then she lights up and tells you all about his red beard, how he taught her the names of the constellations, how he died when she was only thirteen years old, but you get just scraps and fragments until she stops talking and your mom translates the whole thing, and then you wonder what the translation has missed.

Or you are a missionary trying to testify about the atonement, about how the word signifies being made one with God, except that in Spanish the word for *atonement* is *expiación*, which doesn't signify reconciliation and wholeness, at least, not etymologically. So you talk around it, or try to explain how back in the day in England there was this guy named William Tyndale—should we call him Guillermo?—who made up a new word that changes the whole way we understand *la expiación*, that maybe it's not about *expiating* (cleansing, purifying), but instead about something else. But no circumlocution will do. And then one day you begin to wonder if *atonement* really is better than *expiación*, or if your spiritual life is richer for having them both, and if it would be richer still if you understood how Japanese and Quechua and Shona speakers talk about what Christ did for us.

When I asked my mother why she always prays in Spanish, she responded that it feels more intimate to her. It's her true mother tongue and the language she associates with first learning the gospel. There's another reason for that sense of intimacy. In English, we're taught to address God using the archaic pronouns *thee* and *thou* as a sign of respect. In Spanish, we address God using the informal *tú*, rather than the more formal *usted*. We address God the way we would a family member or a friend, rather than a stranger. This is actually equivalent to the English *thee* and *thou*, which formerly indicated familiarity and intimacy, as in the King James Version of the Bible. Here again our spiritual lives become richer in the passage between languages. For a long time I've prayed thinking of the Spanish *tú* and allowing it to charge my *thee* and *thou* pronouns with the static electricity of communion.

Linguistic alienation is frustrating because we tend to think of language as both referential and expressive. It is referential in the sense that we use language to refer to a reality that exists independent of how we communicate, and it is expressive in the sense that we use language to articulate our distinct thoughts and emotions. The breakdown of either of these functions is painful. Growing up, I had a hard time expressing myself to my güelitos in language they could understand, and vice versa. As a missionary, I sometimes felt a gap between the language I possessed and the spiritual reality I wanted to communicate to others.

But here's something a *no sabo* kid knows from an early age: linguistic alienation does not only describe a problem that exists across languages. Linguistic alienation is simply a fact of human experience. It's true that expressing myself to my güelitos was frustrating before I

learned to speak Spanish more fluently. It's also true that expressing myself to my wife in our shared first language of English can sometimes be just as difficult. It's not that I lack words. There are always words. This is one reason we will never exhaust the possibilities of love poems and songs. We are always searching for a new language to express how we feel. And what's more, how we feel is always changing, so we need to find new language to match our evolution as we move through different experiences and stages of life. There are always words, but they never seem to be enough.

Similarly, there will always be a gap between human language and spiritual experience. I feel this most often in prayer, and I rely on Paul's encouraging words in his letter to the Romans: "Likewise the Spirit also helpeth our infirmities: for we know not what we should pray for as we ought: but the Spirit itself maketh intercession for us with groanings which cannot be uttered" (Romans 8:26). Spanish, my mother's tongue, was an imperfect vessel, but so is English, and so is every other language we speak. I'm realizing now as a father that what I heard during those family prayers when I was young was not language, but a yearning that exists beyond language. I hope my children hear it now.

As a former *no sabo* kid I have learned that language is not merely referential and expressive—it is also, and perhaps most importantly, *creative*. I grew up with tíos and tías and cousins who understood this instinctively, who liked to eat a good *lonche* and when you asked where Güelito was, said he was in the bedroom *watcheando* his *novelas*. If I needed my mom to translate for my güelita when I asked her about her father, why was that a loss? Now the stories had to be told twice, shaped and passed through two minds and mouths before arriving in my ears. Now the stories were a room that held four people together—my great-grandfather Refugio, whom I never knew; my güelita Mila, whose eyes shined with her father's memory; my mother, also Mila, who loved to sit close with a hand on Güelita's arm or shoulder; and me, always learning what could and couldn't be said in English, Spanish, or any other language.

Nephi says that after we receive the Holy Ghost we can "speak with the tongue of angels" (2 Ne 32:2), and that he delights in the scriptures so much that his heart "pondereth them, and writeth them for the learning and profit of [his] children" (2 Ne 4:15). Language here isn't only about referring to some preexisting reality, even a reality as urgent as God or the gospel. And if it is about expression, that expression demands new forms. We speak with the tongue of angels, and we ponder what has been written, and we write new truths ourselves. Just as we will never exhaust the possible love songs and poems in our mother tongues, we will never exhaust the potential psalms and praise poems.

Even if we only say the same things over and over again, our language is creative. If we tell our children every day how bad they are at school, if we tell them how lazy they are, we might discover to our chagrin that we have summoned those qualities in them. If we repeat the sentence, "English is the language of the Restoration," to ourselves and others, we contribute to a church in which that ends up being the case. We put the Spanish branch in the basement.

Or, if we say, as I learned to do as a child, "*Te quiero,*" to our grandmother every time we say goodbye, even if we can hardly say anything else in her language, then we create a bond that bridges the divide of linguistic alienation, a relationship that outlasts even her death. If we say, as my mother did ten thousand times when we were growing up, "*Padre Celestial, te pedimos que proteges y cuides a nuestros hijos,*" then even if those *hijos* don't understand the words for *protect* and *care,* even if they don't understand why they need protection or care, we might find we have created through our language a place for them to dwell. And if we can build that small space, surely something bigger is possible—a church with no basement, a cathedral, a city of God where we are no longer strangers. ✶

*Sarah Winegar*

# IN REMEMBRANCE

SUNNY
GRAMES
STIMMLER

AT THE BEGINNING OF 2022, MY husband and I lost two of our closest friends. We knew Jason and Becca when we were all living in Astoria, Queens, in the early 2000s—young newlyweds figuring out jobs and life in New York City. It was a fun and fascinating time. We were part of a large branch full of young, transplanted couples; Bolivians, Peruvians, Greeks, and Filipinos who had called Queens home for decades; and families whose teenage kids had never been to "the city" (Manhattan) just a short subway ride away. Our friendship with Becca and Jason grew around our service in the church. Every Wednesday night we got together with them and a few other friends to watch *The West Wing* as it aired, eating buffalo wings, and talking late into the night. Inevitably, conversation would turn to the people we served in the branch, gospel topics, and issues that both comforted and troubled us as members of the church. Those were formative, precious days—sacred even, as we forged our friendships, identities, and faith. The news of their deaths stunned me, darkening my life in a very real way.

They were killed in a car accident while traveling to a medical conference in Hawaii. In life, they were both changemakers: Becca had led her immigration law firm in offering free legal advice to refugees and migrants at the southern border. Jason changed the world in a quieter way, with a presence, smile, and laugh so comforting that just being near him felt like being hugged. Their deaths—tragic enough for the loss of the extraordinary people they were—felt all the more tragic because of the four children they left behind: siblings they had adopted only a few years previously. When I first heard the news, I immediately thought of the kids, and my heart hurt.

When their funeral came to an end—when all of us who knew them and loved them had said our goodbyes, shared our thoughts, expressed our disbelief, communicated our grief—when all the gathering was over and we went our separate ways, I felt a strong desire to create a way to continue commemorating Becca and Jason, a way to remember them. Not that I would ever fully forget them. I knew their memory would be real and reachable throughout my life—that at any moment I could think about them, remember our time together, recall their influence and impact on me and the world. But I also knew that from day to day, I wouldn't think about them constantly, and eventually, not even frequently. I knew I would return to the routines of life and let go of the grief I felt at their sudden death. I knew I would pick up my life largely as if little had changed and move on from the sadness. And since they had not been a daily presence in my life for over fifteen years, I knew that this would happen quite quickly. I knew that in a very short time, I would forget.

So I felt the need to put in place a ritual—some sort of act that would take place in the same way and the same place and at the same time with regular frequency that would give me reason to pause from routine life and remember them. Something that would summon to my remembrance their personalities, their actions, their contributions, their influence. Something that would commemorate their lives and the loss of them. Something that would symbolize to me my love for them.

In the midst of this yearning, I realized that our weekly sacrament serves this very purpose—providing a regular time, place, and way to remember the Savior—and suddenly a new understanding of the sacrament seemed to open before my eyes. In recent years, a vague idea has flickered in and out of my mind: the sacrament has descended from a ritual first practiced by people who knew the Savior personally. As I listen to the priests pronounce the sacramental prayers every week, the injunction to "remember him" and to eat and drink "in remembrance" of him has caused me to wonder: What did this remembrance mean to those who walked with the Savior? What did commemorating his

80 ≫

WAYFARE

body and his blood feel like to those who had been touched and blessed and healed by him? Undoubtedly, it felt different for them than what I feel each Sunday. But these intimations of understanding never moved beyond small sparks of potential insight; I couldn't quite imagine what it felt like. The reality of the disciples' loss remained a mystery to me until I lost Becca and Jason. The grief I felt at their deaths—the yearning I experienced to remember and honor them over and over—became a gift, an insight allowing me a vision into the beginnings of this practice that marks our most common religious worship.

I imagine the Savior preparing his friends for his upcoming death and departure. He knew that, although they loved him and would grieve over losing him, eventually their grief and sorrow would diminish. Their minds would return to the mundane and worldly. Human nature would make them forget. They would need a way to remember. So he gave them the sacrament. He gave them an act that symbolized him—a practice that gave them emblems, physical reminders of his body and blood, tangible tokens of the way he died, with a broken body and spilled blood. He created a time and a place and a way for them to quietly take into themselves these remembrances. He initiated a routine that would give them a way to commemorate him, honor him, reverence him regularly.

I imagine the Savior's disciples losing him— twice. The first time they lost him, they watched him die. They watched him suffer. The sky darkened. The earth raged enough that even the Roman soldiers cowered and wondered at what had just happened. The disciples saw the Savior's body brutalized. This farewell flowed with blood, reeked of slaughter, and heaved with trauma. The one who was supposed to save them couldn't—or wouldn't—even save himself. But the second time they lost him, they watched as he was carried and received up to heaven. This farewell radiated with light, sang of hope, and resounded with rebirth. Before this farewell, they had watched—initially in terror and alarm—as he spoke to them, walked with them, cooked fish, and then ate with them. At first, they didn't even recognize him, so overwhelming was the experience of seeing alive the

*Ron Richmond*

friend they had just laid to rest. But then their confusion turned to joy and rejoicing as "he took bread, and blessed it, and brake, and gave to them" (Luke 24:30). The very ritual he created to ensure their remembrance of him kindled their recognition of his resurrected self.

Later, as they ate the bread and drank the wine that first time without Jesus, it must have been with a confusing mixture of anguish and awe. Simultaneously, the bread must have summoned images of the mutilated flesh that was his body, while also eliciting the comfort of seeing his body restored to wholeness. The wine must

## What did this remembrance mean to those who walked with the Savior? What did commemorating his body and his blood feel like to those who had been touched and blessed and healed by him?

have awakened memories of blood flowing from and then clotting over his wounds, while also stirring up promises of rebirth and renewal. The act of sharing these sacramental symbols must have recreated the torture of seeing him submit to death, while equally embodying the hopeful miracle of resurrection, healing, and atonement.

I imagine them weeping as they pass the cup and the plate. I imagine the room solemn and still. The act is poignant and personal. They are remembering their friend. This larger-than-life person who swept them up in his miracles and preaching. This master teacher who transformed the way they believed, thought about, and understood everything in life. This person who meant everything to them.

I imagine them introducing the ritual to people who didn't know Jesus. *This represents his body. This represents his blood. He gave himself for us so that we can be healed. He was our friend and greater than anyone we've known. He taught us to love and live in a new way. He changed our hearts.*

*He had the power of God with him, the power to heal any sickness, to raise the dead. And yet, he let himself be arrested, taken, tried, ridiculed, beaten, bruised, and killed. Then he lived again and spoke peace to us once more. We miss him terribly. Our lives are empty without him. So we remember him. We honor him. We memorialize him with this bread and wine.* I imagine them shedding tears as they say this, choking up, needing to pause in their explanation as emotions engulf them and make speaking impossible.

Then eventually, they can perform the ritual without such overwhelming emotion. They feel sadness, but not such deep sorrow. They feel loss, but not such poignant grief. They long for the Savior's presence, but they have made space in their hearts for the loss, blending it into the everyday without letting it go. Now, when they eat the bread and drink the wine, they do so solemnly and with reverence but without the desolation and despair that first marked the custom. They remember, they reflect, they recall.

I imagine them years later with their children, young people who weren't even alive when Jesus was living. They tell stories. They describe his miracles. They tell his parables. They repeat his sermons. And they can do this with smiles on their faces as they remember his goodness and the happiness they felt in his presence. So now, when they participate in the sacrament, they can do so peacefully. Still reverently and quietly, but maybe the act is now touched with gratitude and comfort.

Now when I reach for the bread or cup of water each Sunday, I also reach for the longing to remember that has sprouted in my heart after losing my friends. I let that longing—and the imaginings it has inspired—touch my participation in the sacrament with new emotions. I try to collect those emotions on behalf of the Savior. This isn't a fabrication. This isn't a manufacturing of inauthentic feelings. This is a new understanding. I did not walk with Jesus during his life. I was not a disciple at his feet. I did not know him personally when he lived. But I yearn to feel for him the tangible, palpable love I feel for Jason and Becca. I want my feelings for him to mirror friendship. This evocation of the Savior's friends sharing the bread and wine has transformed the mystery of the sacrament into something

Ron Richmond

more personal, more profound, and more poignant. I am not just going through a motion or completing an impersonal act. I am commemorating a friend.

But in fact, when I return to this ritual every week, I am commemorating more than a friend. I am commemorating my Savior—the one whose death creates life rather than loss. Just like watching Jesus break, bless, and offer bread opened the eyes of the disciples to recognition of their resurrected Savior, so this quest to remember Becca and Jason has opened my eyes and heart to a new recognition of Christ and my love for him. The love I feel for my friends—the hunger I feel to keep their memory alive—is just a shadow of the love I feel for Christ and the reverence I feel for the atonement he suffered on my behalf. Now that love and reverence have been made concrete and tactile, infusing my weekly remembering with new holiness.

I have not created a way to remember Jason and Becca with some kind of ritual. I haven't found something that feels right yet. The ideas that come to mind first feel too religious. In the end, I don't want to venerate my friends as deities; I just want to spend time intentionally remembering them and feeling close to them. I might sit with some of Becca's favorite literature—read a Mary Oliver poem once a month or reread Wallace Stegner's *Crossing to Safety* once a year. I might dedicate a hike with my husband to their memory. I might go back to Astoria every few years and sit on the chapel steps to think about them. Whatever I come up with, my grief has given me a gift. Losing Becca and Jason has offered me something by brightening my understanding of my Savior's sacrifice and the sacrament he gave us to remember it. As I have made this journey to both create a way to ritually remember my friends and understand the feelings of the early disciples, each pursuit has hallowed the other, making sacred the need to remember my friends and casting light on the mystery of the sacrament's essence. The entwining of the two has become its own kind of sacrament in remembrance of my friends. ✳

# TRIALS OF A BAD SPELLOR

*Beyond the Shadow of Judgment*

STEVEN L. PECK

PICTURE A SMALL SIXTH-GRADE boy standing hopefully, expectantly, against a classroom wall. His classmates are lined shoulder to shoulder, faces forward, anticipation and determination garnishing their eager faces. A list of words is proffered down the line, one to each child, who, in turn, must spell back the word in clearly enunciated English. The words are easy at first. In the first pass, none are expected to be asked to sit down. The first group of words is part of the "confidence-building" round. But as the first-round word reaches our young man, he stammers a bit, trying hard, but it is to no avail. He cannot spell it. He is asked to sit. He sits alone for four more passes through every child in the line before the next person joins him at the lonely desks. It is a spelling bee, and our little scholar is always first down, a reminder that he is lacking some aspect of normalcy—he knows he is endowed with a deep flaw that he does not share with his peers.

Alas, the boy is me. I admit this in hopes that my story will inspire others who lack this basic human skill, or perhaps teach such. To be a non-speller in a spelling world is a hard thing. But you need more context. A few more incidents will set the stage for this blight upon my character, but there are some things you must know before I lead you into the depths of my disgrace. First, you must understand that I read voraciously. I always have. By eighth grade, I was reading at a college sophomore level. Second, I love poetry and love to write. A common enough desire, but combine that avocation with a lack of capacity in spelling—that most basic technical skill at the heart of the writing enterprise—and it becomes a tale of tragedy. Or dark comedy, if you are the kind of person who found Hardy's *Jude the Obscure* farcical with its depiction of a poor young man trying to break into the stodgy world of a nineteenth-century British university. For not a few have openly questioned, when confronted with my scribblings, whether I have any facility with written English at all. As an employer said to my father in my senior year of high school, "He is, in fact, functionally illiterate."

There is something monstrous about being different. Let's call it "Unbelonging." A neologism fashioned to capture that sense that one is separate and apart. A flawed thing. Present, but apart. Perhaps uncategorizable. Perhaps shunned. Alone in the presence of others in whatever world they find themselves.

Mary Shelley's *Frankenstein* is a nice place to start looking at what I mean. You need to remember the novel, however. The visual image of the monster that usually comes to mind when Shelley is invoked is the stiff-jointed, flat-topped giant of the 1931 James Whale film, in which the creature is brutish, inhuman, and dimwitted. The creature of the nineteenth-century novel is much different and worth a closer look.

The unnamed creature is thrown into existence as a mélange of decaying human remnants, forming a twisted mereology of embodied mortality. He comes into existence fully conscious but uncertain about what he is and where he fits into the ordered "chain of being" in which he finds himself. It does not take long to learn that he is a horror, despised for the appearance he presents to the world. And which he cannot help.

\*
\*
\* \* ✱
.
.

College freshman English. Our first paper is due. I work hard and turn it in. A friend helps me get the spelling right. Shortly after that, our papers are turned back. All except mine. Lark, my beautiful and elegant graduate student teacher, tells me curtly that I should see her after class. We retreat to her office. I was in love with Lark. We were the same age because I spent time in the army after high school and was, therefore, older than most first-year students. I fancied as I listened, moon-eyed, to her lectures, that in some preexistent state, we must have made certain promises to find one another in this life. It was clear we were meant to be together. Should I ask her out now? She holds up my paper: "I think you plagiarized this." I step back. "Do you know what plagiarism means?" Did she just say that slowly, like

## She holds up my paper: "I think you plagiarized this." I step back. "Do you know what plagiarism means?" Did she just say that slowly, like you would to a dim child? "No, I didn't. I wrote every word," I say. She smirks skeptically, like the Grinch.

you would to a dim child? "No, I didn't. I wrote every word," I say. She smirks skeptically, like the Grinch. "I've seen your in-class essays. You can't write like this." (And it is true, all my in-class essays were returned with loads of the same red circles that many teachers in my life were and will be fond of.) I tell her, "Admittedly, I can't spell. That's all." She says, "If that's true, where did you learn to write like this?"

I'm reaching for anything to redeem myself, and so in desperation, I challenge her, "I've read more books than you have." It is a weak attempt at a stall, but we start a "Have you read this?" contest. It soon becomes apparent that I am not only well read but can hold my own in discussing content and ideas. She finally believes I wrote the piece but decides I need help, and maternally she tells me to enroll in remedial spelling. A 099 level class designed to make up for high school deficiencies. I thank her. I don't ask her out, mostly because I feel unworthy. Flawed. The piece was later submitted to a radio writing contest. I won first place and a fifty-dollar gift certificate to Provo, Utah's finest restaurant. Lark could have shared that meal if things had played out differently. Alas.

*Anna Wright*

The monster and Dr. Frankenstein meet for the first time in the countryside. The monster is miserable and angry: "Everywhere I see bliss from which I alone am irrevocably excluded. I was benevolent and good; misery made me a fiend." He begs for help: "Make me happy, and I shall again be virtuous."[1] Frankenstein, an early archetype of the mad scientist, abandoned his creation in a bout of sickness over what he had created. But here they meet again.

The hideous thing tells his creator its story. It wandered for a time, and slowly, its consciousness became more attuned to the sensations and content of the world. It finds a cozy hovel connected to a rustic cottage in which it can hole up. There, "it" becomes a "he" as he slides into personhood. He makes the little cellar comfortable and tries to figure out where he belongs in the world. A family lives adjacent to his abode. Through listening to their conversations and attending to their habits and concerns, he starts to experience curiosity about the world and pleasure in human company. He helps them discreetly by bringing food or helping to cut the firewood, but he remains hidden from their view, becoming ever more intimate with their history and burdens. He also learns about kindness. He describes how the family gave up their food for the blind old man that lives with them, "This trait of kindness moved me sensibly. I had been accustomed, during the night, to steal a part of their store for my own consumption; but when I found that in doing this I inflicted pain on the cottagers, I abstained, and satisfied myself with berries."[2] He learns to read (with a penchant for Plutarch) and begins to long to become a part of this small group of people he has come to care for. He wants to reveal himself.

I take the spelling class. Under its aegis, I go from about a sixth-grade spelling level to an eighth- or ninth-grade level. It is a triumph. Of sorts. At the same time as I am plugging away at *the most common misspelled words in the English language*, however, tech gurus are inventing WordPerfect—and the spell checker—a prosthetic device that will change my life. Freed at last from the need to pass everything I write to indulgent friends, I can at last make my move. I decide to major in English.

*Anna Wright*

in class lately, afraid of what the future holds. I open the exam, hoping for the best, but there are markings everywhere, like some postmodern art called *red circles and blue lines*. I've flunked. No comment on the content of my writing—only red circles with little "-1s" beside them, each one removing a point from my starting 100. By the end of the exam, I am well into negative numbers. I sit silently through the remainder of class, blinking away the tears trying to escape my eyes. I cannot major in English. I drop the class and the major and wander in darkness for a time, ending finally in that gang of ruffians and ne'er-do-wells who care not a whit about your spelling, as long as you show some flash with a calculator and know how to handle the probabilities: statistics. An unsavory lot, yes, but we take what company we can get.

A dream come true for the kid from Moab, Utah. A win in the university's undergraduate short-story contest has emboldened me. I am feeling daring and empowered. With WordPerfect, no one need ever know my secret shame.

I enroll in a class on English literature prior to 1600 AD. I decide to bypass all the 200-level classes because I've read everything on their lists. The class is mind-blowing, and I am in heaven as we read *Piers the Plowman*, *Canterbury Tales*, *The Song of Roland*. I can't get enough. I am happier than I have ever been. In class, I am Hermione Grangeresque—my hand waving in the air at every opportunity. Then it happens. Our first test is an in-class examination. Blue books. The request that we bring those little stapled notebooks means an essay test. And this would be closed book.

I show up feeling melancholy and afraid. I'm about to be exposed as a fraud, a pretentious charlatan. But who knows? Maybe the teacher will just dock me a few points, and I'll still be fine. I tell myself this over and over. The test comes back after about a week. I've been somewhat subdued

The monster plans his next move carefully. He longs to be a part of the life lived among those in the cottage. He has high hopes. He tells Frankenstein about the pain of his isolation in the hovel where he lives this vicarious life and reveals his plan: "These were the reflections of my hours of despondency and solitude; but when I contemplated the virtues of the cottagers, their amiable and benevolent dispositions, I persuaded myself that when they should become acquainted with my admirations of their virtues, they would compassionate me, and overlook my deformity. Could they turn from their door one, however monstrous, who solicited their compassion and friendship?" Will the villagers see past his hideousness? Can they forget his grotesque and dreadful appearance? Of course. Of course they can.

I discover the subject of ecology and evolution in biology classes, and I start to frame an idea of doing quantitative and evolutionary ecology. Clearly, my days of literature are over. I could not even hear the word "English major" without cringing. I dated one once (an English major, not a "word"), but as with Lark, I felt unworthy in her presence. The relationship could not be sustained—what if she found out about my spelling? If we married, would my refrigerator love notes be covered in red circles?

Well, word processors kept me hidden for the most part. I was discovered from time to time, to my harm and embarrassment, as happened once at UNC–Chapel Hill in my biostatistics program when my Wetlands Ecology professor passed out an in-class essay test. You know what's coming. It was returned with the shaming circles of red branding and highlighting my damnation. He wrote on my paper, "You can't spell. See me!" He was horrified. He told me my problem had its roots in the lack of Greek and Latin in school curricula today. To him, I became a symbol for all that's wrong with twentieth-century education.

Once again, I was reduced to the single dimension of my most significant character flaw. I quit raising my hand in class and started sitting in the back. I quit caring about making an impression and became aloof, cavalier, and supercilious. When he asked for a one-page technical write-up on a wetlands excursion to a nearby lake we had taken, I wrote a four-page narrative poem in iambic pentameter, rhyming words like "zone one census" and "*Impatiens capensis*." He wrote on my paper, "Interesting format. This will do nothing for your career." Sadly, I had asked him before the "spelling incident" to be a recommender for my PhD applications to biology graduate programs. Unfortunately, he sent the letters *after* my exposure as a base-minded scrub. I was accepted to nary a program, despite prior phone calls to my proposed dissertation advisors, who had been enthusiastic when they had only my CV to go on. Something about my letters of recommendation had changed their minds. There was no doubt who sank me and why.

But in math, who cares about spelling? I was free of misjudgment, and math came easily to me.

A bunch of rules and recipes. So I decided to go for a doctorate in biomathematics. Math became a healing drug; *Functional Analysis*, a way to drown the sorrow of failure; proofs, a narcotic for despair. But still, I was bitter, and in secret, late at night, I wrote novels that no one would read and wrote bête noire poems that piled up like scattered Styrofoam containers blown against the cold galvanized steel of a chain-link fence surrounding an inner-city McDonald's. At Christmas each year, I would join in singing with passion, gusto, and pathos the song "We're on the Island of Misfit Toys" as I watched *Rudolph the Red-Nosed Reindeer* with my children. At the appropriate point, I would add to the list of islanders—Charlie-in-the-box, train with square wheels, cowboy riding an ostrich—"a writer who can't spell." Sigh.

The human-made monstrosity decides that he will appeal to the blind old man first while the others are away. Without the ability of the grandfather's eyes to fall on the horrifically dreadful aspects of the poor creature's countenance, perhaps, he imagines, he can slip into his amicable graces without frightening him too much. He enters the cottage by invitation and presents his story and longing to the older man, who bends with kindness towards the miscreation. Just then the sound of footsteps announces the return of the others. He grabs the knees of the old man and begs for protection. The monster describes the events thus: "At that instant the cottage door was opened, and Felix, Safie, and Agatha entered. Who can describe their horror and consternation on beholding me?" [4] Pandemonium follows. The monster is driven violently from the cottage with a stick like a rabid beast. He knows he could destroy his assailants, but he rushes out and returns to his hovel.

The family, who has fled in fear, abandons the cottage permanently. The monster describes the effect on him: "My protectors had departed and had broken the only link that held me to the

# Math became a healing drug; *Functional Analysis*, a way to drown the sorrow of failure; proofs, a narcotic for despair.

world. For the first time the feelings of revenge and hatred filled my bosom and I did not strive to control them; but allowing myself to be borne away by the stream, I bent my mind towards injury and death."[5]

And thus, he becomes the monster of a more familiar mien. Unbelonging. A kind of monster maker. The family could not see beyond what was manifest immediately before them. The surface had become the substance and created anew the substance of their fear *ex nihilo*. The maligned beast would never escape the immediacy of the label that was thrust upon him and that, in the end, became him.

So there you have it. It is only a sketch of my walk as a nonspeller. I'm now a biology professor. I've largely hidden this affliction, but even today, I'm hesitant to write anything on the whiteboard or to put up anything spontaneously that hasn't been vetted through PowerPoint. I can only give a cursory outline of the significant events that amount to thousands of such incidences, losses, and costs. It is a cautionary tale of sorts about the hardness of the world and the snatching of dreams. I don't know why I can't spell or even learn to spell, but if you have critiqued or peer-reviewed any of my papers, you've seen it often enough. I will read and reread things, but the misspellings are invisible to me. My brain reads them as correct, no matter how perverted the spelling. Something deeply embedded in my neurology, still in place despite years of trying to fix it,

*Anna Wright*

is strange and disheartening and speaks of a cold determinism for some things in this world.

Even so, I'm glad to share my shame—if only to convince a few of you to look more closely at that student who seems incorrigibly careless about spelling. Sure, circle a few words just to show you

care, but then focus on what delights might be hiding underneath her tortured salad of symbols. She is not a monster. Maybe she just isn't stitched together quite the right way, and perhaps you can keep her from becoming the maligned creature that the more superficial among us read her to be. ✳

1.  Mary Shelley, *Frankenstein*, Folio Society ed. (London: Folio Society, 2004; originally published 1818), 91.

2.  Shelley, *Frankenstein*, 103.

3.  Shelley, *Frankenstein*, 123.

4.  Shelley, *Frankenstein*, 128.

5.  Shelley, *Frankenstein*, 131.

# CELLAR QUILT

MIKAYLA JOHNSON

i have pieced many quilts in my fifteen years, my fingers calloused and red from the work, my eyes used to tracing careful stitches between separate cuts, used to spreading the fabrics around the livingroom floor and my bedroom floor and the kitchen floor and the back porch deck, because Grandma liked the way it made our floor look like joseph's colored coat or noah's thriving ark, but i've never pieced a quilt down here, in the dark, in Grandma's cellar, my work weaving beneath the watchful eyes of all her carefully placed preserves, jellies and jams and pickles and olives, pears and peaches and onions and beans, their reds and yellows and greens and blacks mirrored in the reds and yellows and greens and blacks of the calico fabrics I snip and place, and it's here that i piece them, place them, cut them, fold them, because down here there's no uncle james to move my cutting board from the table while he talks about choosing foster care, down here there's no aunt marjean to unplug my iron while she tells him they'll lose the money from the will if they do give me up, down here there's no little cousins running through my scrap pile yelling "you can buy a nicer quilt for cheaper at the store, half-brain!", down here there's no older cousins, their paws reaching for the handles of my scissors and the round edge of my rotary blade, holding them to my hair, threatening to cut off my braids if i don't give them the fabric money Grandma pressed into my palm last week, down here is where i do it because before, each time when i handed a finished quilt to Grandma, her eyes lit up, and she pulled it in for a heavy deep breath, and she told me she could smell my pricked fingers and careful placing and midnight sweat, and it smelled like love, she said, and it smelled like me, she said, her golden girl, and she hasn't breathed like that since she fell and broke her spine, and she hasn't smelled like that since her body seized up and died, but maybe, just maybe, since this quilt will wrap her up while she's settled in the grave til kingdom come, maybe this'll be the first thing she breathes in when jesus reaches for her hand, and maybe it'll make her think of me, and maybe she'll ask jesus to reach for me, too, wretched child that i am, because no one's ever wanted me but her, not even mom, and maybe he will take convincing, too. ❋

Artwork by M. Alice Abrams

# BRIEF

JANE
ZWART

For the candle, where the candle
is a proxy for life—flammable
tallow, a taper we trim—there is
no better adjective, though
it doesn't follow that *brief*
is the best word for life.

For one thing, even those
who would impress upon us
the brevity of our turn
favor its synonyms: the poets,
*fleeting*; the evangelists, *short*.
For another, time accordions.

But, yes, brief candles: birthday
cakes staked with wax twigs; dollar
votives that outlive the supplicant;
and apostles, capped with flames.

# SITTING IN THE DARK

DUNCAN
REYBURN

AIR FRANCE'S FLIGHT 447 ON 31 MAY 2009 began normally and ended terribly. I'm told it's not easy to crash an Airbus 330 because of a complicated combination of hardware and software that interfaces pilot-plane interactions. Still, the black box recording of that doomed flight revealed that when all three pilots were faced with a problem not accommodated by the aeroplane's automation, they had no idea what to do to fix it. The interface denied them the possibility of learning how to adapt to a pressing set of unforeseen circumstances. As a result, that enormous airborne tin can was transformed into a monstrous, plummeting deathtrap. Before the plane crashed and killed all 228 people on board, the last words of Captain Pierre-Céderic Bonin, who took charge of the situation and made it worse, were, "But what's happening?"

*What is happening?* We live in an age of *metacrisis.* This is a term for a trend that has been in the works for some time. It's not that we're facing just a few trivial difficulties; rather, we're looking at a simultaneous combination of gigantic, possibly catastrophic crises. War, rumours of war, emigration, the politics of inundation, the politics of incompetence, liberalism twisting and convulsing in postcovidian death throes, democracy failing, policy confusions, religious conflicts, irreligious conflicts, contests around what we're doing to the environment, questions around what the environment is doing to us, and so much more.

Perhaps I'm reading the situation differently than you are. But it seems clear that many of us don't feel so settled and safe hurtling through the world in this plummeting civilisational flying machine. These crises range from the personal to the massively geopolitical. Our problems are material, environmental, economic, psychological, political, spiritual, and religious. "Can you tell me what's wrong with me, doctor?" the Zeitgeist might say to the metaphysical diagnosticians of our time, quivering and nervous, unable to decide which symptoms to disclose first.

Perhaps the formal cause of the metacrisis is modernity itself, which is rooted in a certain sort of consciousness—or perhaps unconsciousness—that frames the world in a certain way to prevent real remedies from being known even as real problems escalate. Modernity has been an interface between us and the world, like the automation of that Air France Airbus. Like the interface of that aircraft, it has become a sort of feedback denial system, preventing the world from getting to us. In particular, modernity has tended to de-halo the world. One term for this, although perhaps misleading, is *disenchantment.* Since the Enlightenment, the divine and spiritual order has been regarded with a skepticism that suggests not quite that there is no supernatural order, but that contact with this order is no longer standard. It has become just one more option on the modern interface.

Unfortunately, since most of us were born into this de-haloing, perception-shaping system, born into a certain pathology of normalcy, it's been difficult to see that it is not the reality, but the mask that hides reality, or the filter that keeps a certain richer view of reality hidden. Like that aeroplane's automation, the visible stuff has hidden the invisible stuff from us. And our failure to attend to the invisible stuff has spelt doom.

Airline safety expert Earl Wiener identifies this critical law in the context of aviation safety: "Digital devices tune out small errors while creating opportunities for large errors." In other words, automation may tidy up ordinary messes, but it'll do so by ignoring all other escalating muddles. I am more than a little tempted to describe a whole host of ways that modernity functions like digital automation. It would be well worth exploring, for instance, how each of its code words—individualism, experimentation, liberation, liberalism, representation, rights, subjectivity, toleration, the nation-state, and so on—have proven poor guides to finding meaning. Nevertheless, I want to focus here only on one tiny little trend, which is, without

*Paul Klee*

a doubt, linked to the artifice of modernity. The trend, evident even in my opening example of aircraft piloting automation, has to do with how we have technologized our lives.

I'm not here to make an irrational blanket judgment on technology. I am well aware of the fact that man is, by nature, driven to develop and work with tools. We are, by divine design, tool-using creatures. There are almost no aspects of our lives that won't be, in often very positive ways, reliant upon some or other kind of technology. I don't think we can live without technology. But what is curious to me, and what I want to highlight, is a certain severe disproportion in

how we have technologized our lives. We apply technological thinking even where it is not or should not be needed. One obvious example is the building I work in.

Designed and built with no thought given to natural ventilation and light, it has such appallingly poor airflow, and even when the world outside is bathed in the most glorious summer light, it is very dark inside without the lights on. Of course, the building is good for quite a lot—it shelters us from the blazing sun and torrential rain. But because it was designed as a shield against natural air and light, certain additional technological interventions have been unavoidable, and air conditioning and electrical light have needed to be added. This architectural deficit is even more problematic because I live in a country, South Africa, with one of the most pronounced energy crises in the world.

I think it is a mistake to cut ourselves off from contact with the world with this disproportionate emphasis on technology. And in addition to this world-alienation, I am concerned mainly with the tendency to render ourselves increasingly passive. One day recently, I arrived at work to find that the power was off. Some of my colleagues were sitting around in the foyer of that dark building doing absolutely nothing. They weren't even talking to each other—they just sat there. One of them smiled at me and shrugged. I wondered if everyone had been unplugged. A question popped into my head: *Why would a failure of electrical power throw so many people into a state approximating mental and physical paralysis?*

Later, I realized that little moment echoed a certain Kierkegaardian insight. Kierkegaard says that when we suffer a loss, it may seem only at first that the loss causes despair. But this is not necessarily the case. He suggests that often we mask our despair by being overly attached to certain things. When we lose those things, the mask is stripped away to reveal a despair that was always there, albeit in an unrecognized form. What Kierkegaard suggests by this is not that it is bad to own things or to rely on things but that we may very well deceive ourselves by relying *too much* on what we claim to own. *Disproportion* is still the issue. What is needed is honesty, stemming from a desire to seek out the truth rather than explain what happens in a way that simply reflects well on us.

It seems to me many of our technologies can function like masks. In the case of finding my colleagues sitting around doing nothing in that dark foyer, the mask was gone. It made me wonder if perhaps I've become accustomed to thinking I'm being active when, in fact, I have succumbed to a passivity that has simply been masked by the tools I use. It is not difficult to *look* busy when sitting behind a computer screen. It is not difficult to *feel* busy when answering a million emails. But is what we busy ourselves with really

## *Acedia* is an inattention to love, a failure to appreciate life itself, and a resistance to the deeper, truer things.

reflective of the full potential of our agency in the world? What does any particular technological mask reveal when it has been stripped away?

I think of Jean-Charles Nault's diagnosis of our time as possessed by what the desert father Evagrius of Ponticus called the noonday devil: *acedia*. The common translation of the term is sloth, but it doesn't get the full import of its meaning quite right. *Acedia* is an inattention to love, a failure to appreciate life itself, and a resistance to the deeper, truer things. Evagrius describes the monk in the grip of the noonday devil as constantly distracted, unable even to pray because he cannot be fully present. Is this what modernity's technological frame encourages? Is this what the interface masks? I think the answer is yes even if we would need to take the trouble individually to look at our lives to figure out how this plays out.

I'm noticing that the technological realm, the typical media ecology we inhabit, sides with rendering us more and more passive, more and more oblivious to how we may be distracting ourselves from the deeper things. Of course, there is a passive component to our being. We are dependent beings through and through. We are dependent upon God, others, and the world. But, once again, it is the disproportion that bugs me when I consider our dependency on technologies. It bugs me to think about the tools we tend to use every day and how they side, by my analysis, with taking our ability to act away from us. I don't mean only that they stop us from doing things ourselves but that they encourage so much distraction, not to mention a fixation on details that may not be so important. We let this happen, too. We submit ourselves to the tools we expect to serve us. They are often our masters when we want them to be our servants. I'm reminded of something Charles Foster writes in his brilliant book *Being a Human* (2021):

We walk in a year what an Upper Palaeolithic hunter would walk in a day, and wonder why our bodies are like putty. We devote to TV brains designed for constant alertness against wolves, and wonder why there's a nagging sense of dissatisfaction. We agree to be led by self-serving sociopaths who wouldn't survive a day in the forest, and wonder why our societies are wretched and our self-esteem low. We, who work best in families and communities of up to 150, elect to live in vast conglomerations, and wonder why we feel alienated. We have guts built for organic berries, organic elk and organic mushrooms, and we wonder why those guts rebel at organophosphates and herbicides. We're homeotherms, and wonder why our whole metabolism goes haywire when we delegate our thermoregulation to buildings. We're wild creatures, designed for constant ecstatic contact with earth, heaven, trees and gods, and wonder why lives built on the premise that we are mere machines, and spent in centrally heated, electronically lit greenhouses, seem sub-optimal. We have brains shaped and expanded, very expensively, for relationality, and wonder why we're unhappy in an economic structure built on the assumption that we're walled islands who do not and should not bleed into one another. We are people who need stories as we need air, and whose only available story is the dreary, demeaning dialectic of the free market.[2]

Foster's examples here point to decisions made, mostly by other people whom we have never met, about how technology might 'help' us. Something similar was noted by G.K. Chesterton years ago—a century ago, in fact—in a series of articles written for *Vanity Fair* under the title *The New Renascence: Thoughts on the Structure of the Future* (1920–1921). You can tell we live in an age of decadence when (almost) everything is outsourced. We pay others to fight for us, entertain us, and rule over us. What would it mean to be less passive, to be more conscious, to be more

## What would it mean if we were to govern ourselves instead of simply outsourcing our lives to our media?

creative, to do more things for ourselves? What would it mean if we were to govern ourselves instead of simply outsourcing our lives to our media? It may be cheap to own a slave but it's still cheaper to be a slave. It is cheaper and more costly at the same time.

What should we do about all of this? I return to my own life, and especially to thinking about South Africa. Global signs of the metacrisis play out in very noticeable ways here in the form of what people talk about as state failure. We've had seriously corrupt politicians run the show for a long time. One of the noticeable consequences of this is that various state-run enterprises, each of which is technological in its own way, have become progressively worse and worse. I've noted the power failures that'll leave people sitting around waiting, doing nothing. But there is, as there always is, another side to this. More and more people in South Africa have been waking up, thanks to so much technological failure, to their capacity to act, to pay attention to what is valuable, to do things for themselves. The number of South Africans moving away from relying on government services in the last few years has been staggering. There's been a shift from public education, electricity, healthcare, policing, public housing, and several other things. Privatisation is the watchword, but perhaps the word is also a mask that functions, like technology, as yet another idea that blinds us to our real situation. The principle is a fundamentally ethical one, captured in a simple question: *What are we responsible for?* To begin with, we are responsible for what we attend to and how we attend to it. We can seek humility and stand in awe of the many gifts given to us in the world around us.

I am not suggesting anything like Luddism. I am suggesting, rather, that it is worth taking time to wonder if and how the tools we use may be masking something, and especially whether they may distract us from the deeper things. I'm suggesting that we can become more mindful, more alert, to our own capacity to act. It is quite instructive to notice when we should pick our tools up or put them down, just so that the mere force of technological habit, by sheer automation, does not have the final say over the shape of our lives. It is helpful to notice whether we have allowed ourselves to be conditioned to believe that what our tools demand of us is what matters most just so that we can alter how we operate in the world. The media guru Marshall McLuhan put what I'm trying to say better than I can: "There is no inevitability as long as there is a willingness to contemplate what is happening."[3]

We can change our minds instead of sitting around in the dark. In fact, I'm just here to remind you, and me too, that every time we use a tool, every time we submit ourselves to certain technological mediations, we are making a choice. Maybe we forget that we are making a choice, as we assume too easily that we must merely conform to what is handed to us. But this is not how it is. Evagrius would say that combating the noonday devil means persevering in what is good, including in prayer; taking time to meditate on scripture, as we realign ourselves to what is ultimate; repenting of those mental

and physical habits that cast a shadow of unreality over all we think and do; and labouring with greater intentionality. We are not under any obligation to go the way of that doomed Airbus, if a dramatic metaphor may be allowed. This is something Chesterton reminds us of in one of the best critiques of modernity out there, from his book *The Outline of Sanity* (1928), and it is with this little thought that I want to leave you:

> The aim of human polity is human happiness. . . . There is no obligation on us to be richer, or busier, or more efficient, or more productive, or more progressive, or in any way worldlier or wealthier, if it does not make us happier. Mankind has as much right to scrap its machinery and live on the land, if he really likes it better, as any man has to sell his old bicycle and go for a walk, if he likes that better. It is obvious that the walk will be slower; but he has no duty to be fast.[4] ✳

1. "Wiener's Laws," Aviation Week, July 28, 2013.

2. Charles Foster, *Being a Human: Adventures in Forty Thousand Years of Consciousness* (New York: Metropolitan Books, 2021), 6–7.

3. Marshall McLuhan and Quentin Fiore, *The Medium is the Massage* (London: Bantam, 1967), 25.

*Paul Klee*

# CHAOS, CREATION, & SPIRIT

*Surrendering to God at the Edge of Order*

**GREER BATES CORDNER**

THE FIRST ACT OF CREATION IN the Hebrew Bible is the rush of Spirit into a "formless void." Before God whispered light into being, or split the water from dry land, or watched organisms form and swarm until each habitat on earth teemed with creeping, flapping, swimming life, Spirit flooded chaos.

The text doesn't indicate what Spirit *did* to the chaotic matter, although Bible scholars and lay readers have formed theories about Spirit's role in creation, ranging from Spirit as "life-giver," as "communicator," or as "the power of creativity."[1] In general, these theologies tend to portray creation as an ordering of chaos, and cast Spirit as God overcoming disorder. "By the work of the hovering Spirit," one Baptist theologian wrote, "God is going to tame the darkness and the water of the chaotic earth and bring forth life of many kinds."[2] *Tameness* and *order* therefore emerge as the hallmarks of Spirit, and as the purpose of creation.

For their part, Latter-day Saints have typically followed this strain of theology, characterizing creation as an act of "organization" (Abraham 4) by which order emerged from chaos. In LDS theologies of creation, the apex of this "organization" occurred with the formation of physical bodies for God's spirit-children (humankind). Unlike most of their fellow Christians, Latter-day Saints also celebrate the so-called "Fall" as a necessary step that enabled the First Couple to "ha[ve] seed" (Moses 5:11). Human procreation then becomes an extension of God's greatest act of creation, and everyone who participates in it gets the honorifics "mother" or "father"—titles they share with the Heavenly Parents that Latter-day Saints revere. Thus, human bodies emerge as part of God's organizational work, and human families become the organizational unit of the "plan of salvation." Latter-day Saints have good reason to place a theological premium on bodies and families, especially since many of the unique claims within LDS theology relate to the eternality of physical bodies and family bonds.

But too much focus on *order* and *organization* can distract from important theological complexities—especially those related to Spirit. Mark Galli argues that "[c]haos is the work of the Spirit. . . . Chaos reveals the excessive order and forces us to make a decision—either to grasp ever harder [for] control or to let our lives be led by the Spirit."[3] Galli's observation highlights the fact that Spirit's work in the world is not always orderly; Spirit does, in fact, seem comfortable in chaos. Spirit *rushed* into chaos before the earth formed, and history and scripture document the ways Spirit sparked chaos in charismatic outbursts of worship, overpowering bodies to flail or

# Spirit's work in the world is not always orderly; Spirit does, in fact, seem comfortable in chaos.

collapse (Alma 18–19) or speak in ways that made onlookers suspect drunkenness (Acts 2:15). For Latter-day Saints in particular, Spirit challenges order. After all, unlike the other members of the Godhead in LDS theology, Spirit lacks both a physical body and titles that correlate to human relationships, making it difficult to square Spirit with ideals about bodies and families in eternal plans.

This ambiguity of Spirit opens possibilities for theological work into other ways that life departs from order and ideals—including disability. Christian theologians have long wrestled with tensions that arise from the lived experiences of individuals whose bodies and families do not fully square with doctrines. For instance, Sharon Betcher has pointed out that "[i]n theology, Spirit has often been made the agent of . . . Final Perfection," in which perceived impurities and imperfections dissipate.[4] Sometimes this mentality falls victim to a binary of *wholeness* and *brokenness*, which rewards "performance of the ideal," the orderly, the complete.[5] Betcher—who lost a leg in an emergency amputation—notes that Christian theology often lacks full engagement with disabled bodies, favoring accounts of healing and other miraculous restorations of "wholeness" above grappling with bodies that remain "broken."[6] Candida Moss and Joel Baden likewise have observed religious stigmas around infertility, especially in communities that view procreation as part of the "natural order" by which humans fulfill God's commandment to "be fruitful and multiply."[7] Infertility, like other disabilities, transgresses theological ideals about order in physical bodies and in family structures.

Latter-day Saints pattern the ideal family—father, mother, children—after theological tenets, and performance of that ideal translates into norms and assumptions in LDS culture. Not every Latter-day Saint can perform that ideal, however, for myriad reasons that warrant attention. As a straight woman who married in her mid-twenties, though, I was privileged to assume that the cultural norms I breathed since childhood would match my reality. I certainly never assumed that the thing I'd been taught was one of the greatest gifts God gave me—my reasonably healthy body—could prevent my performance of the theological ideal I'd learned to see as my part in God's ongoing creation.

I received the first of what became a series of diagnoses contributing to infertility during the second semester of my master's program. Achieving that diagnosis had required not only a handful of doctor's visits and blood tests, but also an MRI that occurred the day before an important exam in my New Testament class. As I frantically shuffled through flashcards on the bus to the hospital for the procedure, I wondered whether the imaging techs could read the cards to me while rays scanned my brain for a tumor on my pituitary gland. (I didn't realize that the machine's noise would make that impossible.) I also wondered whether I'd retain anything I studied, since all I could think about was the way my life's vision was fading.

As the second oldest of my parents' eleven kids, I had no frame of reference for infertility. I had changed diapers for and fed bottles to babies as long as I could remember. And before we married I had confessed to my now-husband that I hoped our family might look something like the one that I grew up in. In fact, I'm pretty sure I used that classic phrase, "accept any children God sends us" (obviously meaning lots), and Nathan was on board.

We moved across the country soon after our wedding so that I could begin a degree in theology, and when my period disappeared I assumed, first, that I was pregnant. After a negative test, I then

*Carly White*

assumed that three huge life changes in quick succession—marriage, move, and grad school—had simply overstressed my body. Months later, though, my period remained missing, and Nathan and I had hit the minimum threshold for infertility, so I phoned the student health center.

Workup procedures, specialist visits, follow-up MRIS, and medications consumed another full year, and during that time I began to realize that being a big-family mom—Plan A for my life—might not happen. In tears one night during prayer, I began to consider Plan B: more schooling. By the time Nathan and I had secured additional infertility diagnoses, we had also both secured offers for doctoral programs.

Within the first few years of marriage, then, infertility forced me to reexamine my theological assumptions—especially as an LDS woman—in light of "disorder" inside my body and my life. I had grown up around many strong, fulfilled stay-at-home mothers; I had not grown up around many women who got PhDs. At church gatherings, Nathan and I often fielded the question, "How many kids do you have?" (taking for granted there would be some), and when we said, "None, yet," we usually met the response, "Well, you're both busy with school," as if that were why. The first time I attended a Mormon History Association conference, a fellow presenter who learned I didn't have kids said, "Good—it's hard to be a student-parent. You're smart to wait till you're done."

"Well, it isn't by choice," I confessed.

He looked away quickly. "Oh. I'm sorry to hear that."

So was I.

The questions and assumptions stung, but didn't surprise me. After all, choice, or agency, is also a theological focal point for Latter-day

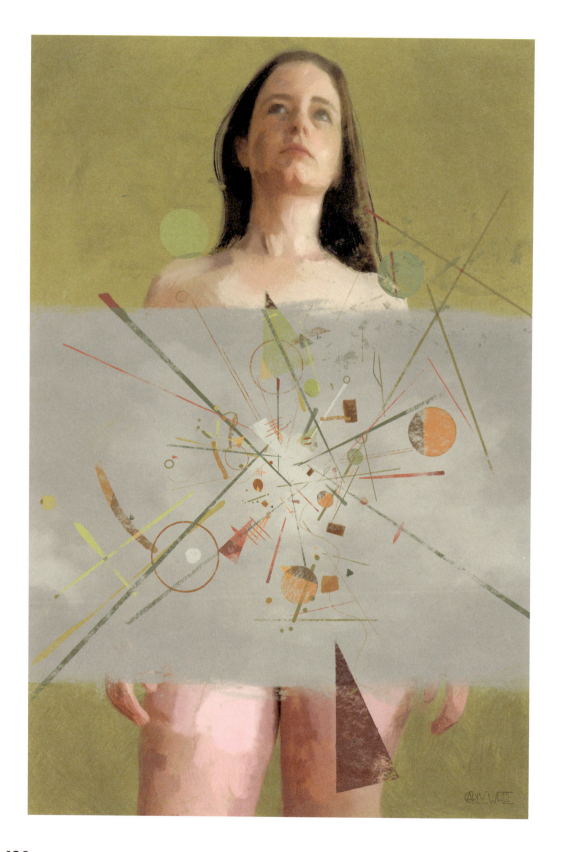

Saints, and another integral part of our creation narratives. In an account unique to Latter-day Saints, God's decision to make "an earth whereon [people] may dwell" stemmed from his desire to "prove" his spirit-children, observing what choices they would make (Abraham 3:24–25). It wasn't until Adam and Eve asserted agency that they became able to conceive (Moses 5:11), so creation as a whole, and creation of individual bodies in particular, all bind our theology of procreation to our theology of choice.

Language of agency also permeates the way American society discusses childbearing (think "family *planning*," or "birth *control*"). Infertile people—though not rare—are a social minority, and because options do exist for individuals and couples to engineer their families in line with their choices, Moss and Baden note that the "default assumption [tends] to be that childless couples have simply made a lifestyle choice." That assumption carries different weight in different contexts, but in religious communities that prioritize marriage and family, that cast procreation as co-creation with God, and that emphasize agency, a social stigma often accompanies childlessness.

Infertile Latter-day Saint couples shoulder an invisible disability, a physical "disorder" that affects their participation in cultural norms and participation in God's "work and glory" (Moses 1:39). Childbearing, for them, is no matter of agency. They wait, and they pray, not as things to act but as things to be acted upon (2 Nephi 2:13)—at least in this critical sphere.

\* \* \* \* \* \* \*

While I waited, I studied, although I never intended my schoolwork to yield insight into my personal life. Drawing on questions that had fomented during my master's program, I dived into research about ways American Christians have understood and experienced Spirit, and how those experiences changed over time. In the accounts of Methodists, Presbyterians, Baptists, and others, a pattern struck me: Charismatic revivals and conversions characterized many early stories, but eventually fell away to routine, institutionalization, and order.[8] In early revivals, worshipers often lost control of their bodies to Spirit, moving and speaking in ways they didn't choose. Later, church leaders warned against such outbursts, imposing a "respectability" that recognized Spirit only in certain acceptable manifestations.

As numerous scholars have observed, Latter-day Saints followed a similar trend, attempting to rein in the chaos of Spirit.[9] During the nineteenth century, many of the ecstatic expressions of Spirit that characterized early LDS worship lost place, in favor of a staid tone that equated *quietness* with *reverence*. Tongue-speaking turned into a tool for missionary language acquisition, instead of a spontaneous outburst in chapels. Healing accrued ritual performed only by ordained men instead of any person of faith. The company one keeps, the music one listens to, even the cleanliness of one's home all affect one's ability to "have the Spirit," in common LDS rhetoric. Each step emphasized *order* and *organization* as spiritual ideals.

And yet, despite efforts to define, describe, and detail Spirit within institutional routines, there remain far too many aspects of Spirit that are just out of reach—a God with no physical body, who can "dwell in us" (Doctrine and Covenants 130:22), overtake our dreams, thoughts, and language, cause convulsions, change plans, and change hearts.

It remains difficult to square Spirit within doctrines of bodies and agency and order. But this can be good news for individuals whose own bodies veer from cultural norms, who lack control in their lives, who wrestle with uncertainty and grasp for something familiar and fleshy and firm. In the "formless void" of infertility—or any other void that engulfs us—*Spirit is there*. Spirit sanctifies disorder and chaos. Spirit acts beyond our own agency. Long before there is light, there is Spirit—and Spirit remains in the chaos of creation.

Nathan and I have welcomed miracle babies into our family—something that seemed, for years, unlikely. There is no medical reason why conception evaded us and then, abruptly, did not. Nothing changed in my body; its disorders remain. And although we now perform some of the cultural norms about LDS families, we still challenge

*Carly White*

others, partly due to ways our lives and goals changed through our infertility. When we married, we didn't expect to become dual academics, balancing teaching and research schedules with trips to the playground and nap duty. We've loosened our grip, faced the limits of our choices, and seen messy miracles that have taken our lives in directions we couldn't have planned. But I'm coming to believe that *that* is the hallmark of Spirit: creation emerging from chaos in ways that escape our powers of control and description. ✱

1. Jürgen Moltmann's concept of Spirit as "life-giver" arises in his book *God in Creation* and forms the crux of David Beck's analysis of Moltmann's pneumatological creation theories in *The Holy Spirit and the Renewal of All Things: Pneumatology in Paul and Jürgen Moltmann* (Cambridge: James Clarke & Co., 2010), 207–27. Sjoerd Bonting proposes the idea of Spirit as "God the Communicator"—notably since scripture portrays God *speaking* the world into being through creation—in his article "Spirit and Creation," *Zygon* 41, no. 3 (September 2006): 713–25. Reading Spirit as "the power of creativity" is Clark Pinnock's approach in "The Role of the Spirit in Creation," *The Asbury Theological Journal* 52, no. 1 (Spring 1997): 47–53.

2. Kyle Claunch, "In the Beginning Was the Spirit: The Third Person in Genesis 1," Desiring God, April 16, 2022.

3. Mark Galli, *Chaos and Grace: Discovering the Liberating Work of the Holy Spirit* (Grand Rapids: Baker Books, 2011), 91.

4. Sharon V. Betcher, *Spirit and the Politics of Disablement* (Minneapolis: Fortress Press, 2007), 3.

5. Betcher, *Spirit and Disablement,* 5.

6. Betcher, *Spirit and Disablement,* 5, 25.

7. Candida Moss and Joel Baden, *Reconceiving Infertility: Biblical Perspectives on Procreation and Childlessness* (Princeton: Princeton University Press, 2015), 12, 17.

8. Nathan Hatch's *The Democratization of American Christianity* (New Haven: Yale University Press, 1989) provides a classic overview of this trend, and other scholars (like John Wigger in *Taking Heaven by Storm: Methodism and the Rise of Popular Christianity in America* [Urbana: University of Illinois Press, 1998]) make similar arguments.

9. For example, see Armand L. Mauss, "Culture, Charisma, and Change: Reflections on Mormon Temple Worship," *Dialogue* 20, no. 4 (Winter 1987): 77–83; Thomas Alexander, *Mormonism in Transition: A History of the Latter-day Saints, 1890–1930* (Urbana: University of Illinois Press, 1996); and the theme is also addressed (albeit briefly) in Hatch, *Democratization of American Christianity.*

# EASTWARD

D.A.
COOPER

The steamship dies just short of Paradise
where fog erases shores left far behind.
Heeding the siren's call comes at a price:

the gentle ripping, tearing of the mind.
While floating there beneath the burning moon,
the fog erases shores we left behind,

where ancient children danced and sang a tune
to cosmic melodies we couldn't hear.
While sailing eastward toward the rising moon,

we watch as refugees from life appear,
they dance with clacking heels and clapping hands
to cosmic melodies we still can't hear.

As frenzied revelry for death expands,
the ashen ocean shudders in delight.
We dance and clack our heels and clap our hands

as unknown woodwinds play into the night.
We lie in port just short of Paradise,
while crystal oceans croon under the light
and weep for those who cannot pay the price.

# A CAREFUL MENDING OF THE WORLD

*The Creative Work of Hope*

PAIGE CROSLAND ANDERSON

SUFFERING ABOUNDS. THIS WE all know. When a longtime friend unexpectedly lost her sister—the only family she had in the faraway state in which she lived, and on the heels of her father's passing—my heart was broken and my hands felt impotent. What could I possibly do to ease her suffering?

Lehi taught his sons, and us, that the reality of suffering enables the duality of joy and sorrow. Curiously, however, to begin his discourse on suffering and redemption, he starts at the Creation. As he describes the creation of the fowls, the beasts, and our first parents, "the heavens and the earth, and all things that in them are,"[1] I am reminded that the Creation story ends with a command to *do*. Continue His creative work by creating. The Lord tells His people to go forth and "to dress [this garden] and to keep it."[2] The command seems to foreshadow the ongoing repair that would soon be required by this newly fallen world.

In Ecclesiastes, the command to create is reiterated: "Whatsoever thy hand findeth to do, do it with thy might; for there is no work, nor device, nor knowledge, nor wisdom, in the grave, whither thou goest."[3] I sense an urgency in those words that seem to recognize that the needs we see will go beyond our hands' ability to aid before we return to dust. There is so much to do. Engage in this careful mending however you can and meet the suffering you see with ready hands, the Ecclesiastical preacher seems to implore. "Do it with thy might," he says. As Latter-day Saints, we are even covenantally bound to mourn with those that mourn, to knit our aching hearts to theirs, to stitch the suffering world back together.

A friend introduced me to a Jewish concept that encapsulates all this. It both fascinates and inspires me. *Tikkun olam* refers to the ongoing act of repairing the world.[4] To me, this repair implies the need for creation. We believe that even the creation of our world was a refashioning of existing elements. Our own creative efforts come in the form of gathering in what we see around us— the broken, disparate bits—and making something that speaks to wholeness. *Tikkun olam* recognizes that the world is full of brokenness, and it also acknowledges that humans can participate in small acts of repair that bring newness and wholeness to what was once broken.

I love to think of creation in its many forms as many acts of healing repair. It is a hopeful thought that though my efforts are meager when compared to the magnitude of sorrow I see, somehow, someway, my small acts of creation are able to reverberate outward—contributing to a greater wholeness. I am inspired when I think of creative work as holy work.

The definition of "holy" as offered by Jewish scholar Jacob Milgrom is beautiful in its piercing simplicity: Holiness means imitating God.[5] It's almost too simple, isn't it? Holiness means imitating God. But as I contemplate God's command to dress this garden, the Jewish concept of repairing the world, and the Ecclesiastes charge to do with might, I am struck with clarity of purpose: *be a creator.*

Milgrom says *holiness* is "that which humanity is commanded to emulate and approximate."[6] Revealing the hand of the Creator through our own acts of creation seems like a good step toward approximating this holiness. When I am making, I feel the spark of the divine in me. I feel the memory of learning to mimic my Father as I approximate His ways and seek to be like Him. I relate closely to what famed author Madeleine L'Engle says about her feelings when she listens to music by Johann Sebastian Bach: "Bach's music points me to wholeness, a wholeness of body, mind, and spirit, which we seldom glimpse, but which we are intended to know. It is no coincidence that the root word of *whole, health, heal, holy, is hale* (as in hale and hearty.) If we are healed, we become whole; we are hale and hearty; we are holy."[7]

Creative work is holy work. It is repairing-to-make-whole work. It is sometimes the only work my hands know to do when all around me feels in chaos and despair. We must acknowledge that sometimes the needs we see are far beyond the scale of any two hands. But where does that reality leave willing hands that cannot find a way to do much of anything that feels consequential?

In addition to the suffering I saw in my friend, I saw suffering spilling from newspaper headlines and social media feeds, war and divisiveness further wounding a wounded world. I had willing hands that frequently found themselves clasped in prayer. "What can my hands do?" I asked.

I remembered a 2022 Facebook post that American author Anne Lamott wrote about the stunningly unnecessary beauty of springtime

*Paige Crosland Anderson*

and how simply bearing witness to these small beauties can affect the world. She wrote, "In 68 years, I have never seen a boring sky. I have never felt blasé about the moon, or birdsong, or paper

whites. It is a crazy drunken clown college outside our windows now, almost too much beauty and renewal to take in. The world is warming up." She goes on, "Well, how does us appreciating spring help the people of Ukraine? If we believe in chaos theory, and the butterfly effect, that the flapping of a Monarch's wings near my home can lead to a weather change in Tokyo, then maybe noticing beauty—flapping our wings with amazement—changes things in ways we cannot begin to imagine. It means goodness is quantum. Even to help the small world helps. Even prayer, which can seem to do nothing. Everything is connected."[8]

And so my time in the studio became a near-constant prayer. Words to ancient hymns came to my mind. I sang them out loud in an empty house as a form of invocation, hoping somehow the music and message would be winged across the country on the back of a prayer meant to bring a measure of peace. I looked and listened for every divine spark and tried to use it to make a tender flame of hope and comfort. Rabbi Isaac Luria taught that our job "is to find those divine sparks, select them, and reconnect them to their original, higher purpose. . . . How do we find those sparks? Simply by doing those same activities, but in a way that reveals a higher, divine meaning."[9] Rabbi Tzvi Freeman concludes that "Each tikkun has the potential to change everything." My *tikkun* in those moments became the only thing I could find to do with my hands in the face of immense and faraway suffering: clasp them and pray mightily. It was a small, but hopeful, creative act.

I'm a believer that creative acts can begin by digging into the mundane. It is only through constant daily re-creation that the world is transformed. The reality is that we cannot live outside the world. We are bound by the dailiness of feeding, sleeping, caring, and cleaning. The Mishnah teaches that "each person is an entire world" and any improving act made within a person reverberates, a bit like the butterfly effect described by Lamott, through the rest of the world. Divine creation must begin with the ordinary. After all, didn't the Holy One of Israel have an ordinary upbringing, live in an ordinary town, and have to fill his life with the ordinary rhythms of mortality too? So that must be where our pressing calls to *do* and to *create* arise from.

The work of bringing wholeness to the world is grounded in living in the world. *Whatsoever thy hand findeth to do, do it with thy might.* My hands are most often found, in my little world, in the near-constant care of young children. *Do it with thy might.* I wake them, help them dress, brush their hair, my hands on their heads like a blessing. Time for breakfast. *Whatsoever thy hand findeth to do . . .* I prepare food, help with last-minute shoes, papers, signed reading logs, lunches, and backpacks . . . *do it with thy might.* I walk them to school. This is holy work? It is the pressing work before me. It is creating hale and hearty children. It is leading to whole lives that are full. It is demanding and creative. It requires constant attention and careful repair. Mistakes are made in abundance, but so are efforts at restoration. This is holy work.

A month after her sister's passing, I texted my friend: "Thinking of you today. I hope your heavy heart has found moments of lightness during the past month. Even though Christmas is over, I can't seem to get 'O Come, O Come, Emmanuel' out of my head. There is so much long, dark winter ahead." Wave upon wave of crashing sorrows continue. Darkness and brokenness persist. And so too does our call to "do with might" the many acts of repair ahead of us, as we participate in the holy work of creating a world that is whole.

"Rejoice! Rejoice! Emmanuel
    shall come to you, O Israel."[10] ✳

1.    2 Nephi 2:14.

2.    Genesis 2:15.

3.    Ecclesiastes 9:10.

4.    Tzvi Freeman, "What Is Tikkun Olam?," Chabad.org, accessed May 25, 2024.

5.    Jacob Milgrom, *Leviticus: A Book of Ritual and Ethics* (Minneapolis: Fortress Press, 2004), 107.

6.    Milgrom, *Leviticus*, 107.

7.    Madeleine L'Engle, *Walking on Water: Reflections on Faith and Art* (New York: Convergent Books, 1980), 60.

8.    Anne Lamott, "I am going to be 68 in six days," Facebook, April 5, 2022.

9.    This and the two quotes that follow are from Freeman, "What Is Tikkun Olam?"

10.   William Henry Monk, ed., *Hymns, Ancient and Modern, for Use in the Services of the Church* (London: J. Alfred Novello, 1861), hymn 36.

# MYSTERY & FAITH

MARJORIE
PERRY

It was logical to be agnostic. There was no data, no proof to back up faith in the supernatural, the divine. I wanted to believe, but you can't choose to believe, can you? I couldn't.

Growing up, I'd been raised to believe in God (or should I say, "a God"?). The rudimentary conception was there was someone out there, a benevolent force who cared. They were concerned with how your life was going, but mostly let you steer. But if the show went way off script, things went haywire, they might pull the emergency brake for you, maybe? They were a friend you'd never met. You prayed to them, and searched for signs of a reply.

In my family, we didn't discuss God. My mom didn't make any supplications in front of us. Sunday mornings were for church; Monday evenings were for youth Bible study. Before supper, we prayed. Before sleep, my father came in and said prayers with me, encouraging me to add names of people who needed help.

After completing the Bible study program in eighth grade, I was confirmed. Sister Anna and I had a brief conversation in the church rectory. Facing one another, with feet flat on the floor, we sat in blue plastic chairs with thin silver legs. What we discussed, I don't recall. Whatever I'd said, it was sufficient, I was pronounced confirmed.

Several years later, faith, or even the contemplation of the nonmaterial, disappeared from my life. Materialism made sense. Why should there be anything more than this physical universe? There was no data, no science, no experiments to convince me otherwise. No hotline to reach a mysterious God; no ladder to find heaven. My arms were too short to reach God, and legs too tired to make that leap of faith.

This line of thought rolled on for decades.

But then, a year ago, there was a series of inexplicable experiences that changed my mind. I've run the memories through my mind countless times, seeking a reasonable, scientific explanation for them.

It was my birthday; I was enjoying the sun in a park on the Lower East Side. An older Black man

## My arms were too short to reach God, and legs too tired to make that leap of faith.

approached me and struck up a conversation. Perhaps due to my journalism background, I'm comfortable talking with strangers. He appeared homeless and nonthreatening. The conversation was light and polite.

Then it was time for me to move on. The man, who'd introduced himself as Kareem, said he was headed in the same direction. Several minutes later, we reached a point where our paths diverged.

He turned to me and said, "I might try to come to tell you something sometime."

Huh? I didn't understand what this meant. "How would I know?" I asked.

"You'll know by the sound of my voice," he said.

I didn't know what to think. But I was curious enough. I suggested we exchange numbers; we did. And we went separate ways. In the following weeks, he didn't message me, nor I him. Kareem never asked for money, or any kind of help for that matter. So that was that.

Who knows why people say what they do? Perhaps he wanted attention or the feeling of human connection. While in college, I had spent a week volunteering at homeless shelters and soup kitchens. Part of that experience was doing an "urban plunge," where for forty-eight hours I lived as a homeless person. The thing that struck me most was how quickly you become invisible. I couldn't fault Kareem for being theatrical. It was a good strategy to stay sane.

Several weeks passed and I had the most powerful dream of my life thus far. A Black man appeared and stood several feet in front me. There was no backdrop in the dream, no scenery, and no sequence that led to it. Out of darkness and from nothing, there he was.

Whether he spoke, or I heard him with my mind, I'm not sure. But the message was clear, solid, and defined.

A single line: "God said you'll always be OK."

Instantly, I bolted upright from the dream, sobbing. In shock, I poured down the stairs into the kitchen and dropped to the floor, on my knees. My body was electric. The room was still and dark and quiet.

My roommate came downstairs, I'd woken her up. I told her my dream. We stood in silence.

It was almost 6 a.m., and I was too hyped up to sleep. So I went to the grocery store to get breakfast. I stood in the neon-lit aisle, feeling half-real, pondering whether I should get Cap'n Crunch, Honeycomb, or Corn Pops.

My phone pinged green, and there was a text from Kareem.

"How are you this morning?" he asked.

"I'm good, sir, how are you?"

"Remember you're not just good. You're great. Because God is great."

Am I awake? What *is* awake? There is no thinking. I brought home three cereal boxes.

Later I told my mom this story. The story of the man coming up to me in the park on my birthday, and then telling me he is going to tell me something; and then having the dream, and then the text from Kareem, and if anyone could or should tell you the truth, it would be your mom, right?

My mom said that several years ago she took a meditation course. When the class was finished, the teacher gave each student a mantra word. My mom's word? Kareem.

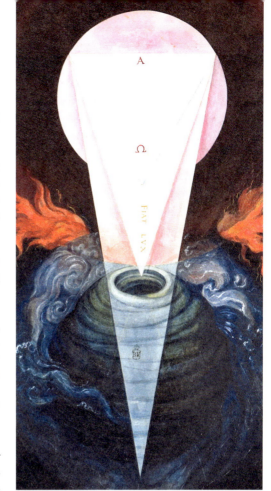

*Francisco de Holanda*

I'd never met anyone named "Kareem," nor had my mom. The name comes from Arabic, and is translated as "generous," as well as "dignified" and "dignity." In the Quran, it is one of the attributes given to Allah (the Lord). As al-kareem, he is described as "The Most Generous One."

In the Bible, the Book of Luke mentions the birthplace of John the Baptist, which scholars suggest was the town of Ein Karem (alternative spelling: Ain Karem).

The sequence of events doesn't make sense. They seem connected, but how *could* that be? Some days I mull over these events and wave them all off. Other days I think it's the most magical thing that's ever happened to me, and I'm stunned to think I could be worthy of a reassuring word from God.

Several weeks later I was sitting at a coffee shop in Brooklyn. It was a gray day with intermittent rain that raced across the tall windows. The question kept nagging at me—had these events been sublime or merely sequential?

I wrote down the synchronicities I'd experienced. Was there a pattern, some unseen force behind the sequence, or was my mind drawing connections where there were none?

A few feet away, near the cash register, there was a young guy with short brunette hair and bright brown eyes. He was standing there, looking at me, and I looked up at him.

"God has a very special love for you," he said.

My jaw went slack. I waved for him to come over and showed him my notebook. At the top of the page: "Ways God has spoken to me?"

This stranger and me, we threw our heads back and laughed. We high-fived. We were awestruck. When I interviewed him for this piece, he recalled that when he first saw me, "it was like there was a highlighter over you, saying how special you are to God."

Walking to the train, I waltzed through the rain. There is no amount of money, no level of prestige, nothing that one could acquire or accumulate here on Earth that is better than this feeling—that an eternal, divine, benevolent God sees you and cares for you.

I felt profoundly content & wanted for nothing.

These experiences required me to revisit long-held assumptions about how the world works and the function of my existence in this world.

In mulling over these events, I kept coming back to mathematical probability. What is the probability of meeting a man named Kareem, who says he will "tell me something," who then texts me in the early morning after a powerful dream? And then the probability for my mom to have a connection to this word? Or, in the following weeks, to be questioning this series of events, to have a stranger blurt out "God has a special love for you"?

These things seemed too coincidental to be mere coincidence, too interconnected to have arisen from pure chance.

Carl Jung, a Swiss psychiatrist and psychoanalyst, popularized the concept of "synchronicities." Jung defined these as circumstances or events that appear meaningfully related yet lack a causal connection. An example often cited to illustrate this concept comes from a therapy session, which Jung wrote about in *Synchronicity* (1973). Jung's patient was recounting a dream about a golden scarab. At this moment, a yellow beetle was buzzing outside, knocking itself on the window of their room. Jung opened the window and the beetle flew in. He noted that it was not the season for this insect, and this was atypical behavior.

According to Newtonian physics, the prevailing paradigm for the last three centuries, the physical world is governed by cause and effect. Like billiard balls on the green wool of a pool table, our visible world is discrete and sequential—the cue strikes the ball, which propels it forward, knocking into another, which carries on in its own trajectory. A causes B, and the linkage is clear.

According to Newtonian physics, it makes no sense for the recounting of a dream to result in changes in insect behavior. Or for the two to have any kind of relationship whatsoever. There is no physical linkage between the dream and the beetle; the dream did not summon the beetle. And yet somehow, in our minds—or at least in Jung's mind—they have some kind of connection.

The closest physical science we have to synchronicity is quantum entanglement. In 2022, the Nobel Prize in physics was awarded to scientists who demonstrated this phenomenon. Their experiments showed that the physical world is not entirely explainable by Newtonian physics. At another level of measurement, a different model is required. In that realm, particles can affect each other instantaneously across enormous distances. This goes against the Newtonian model of cause and effect, and the restrictions of spacetime.

For me, a fantastical dream was haloed by people, statements, and synchronicities that appear to underscore its veracity. This does not make sense. It is not logical.

My own life defies my ability to understand it, and there are scant options to verify or refute different interpretations. Yet, we learn from and are influenced by all of our experiences. My insistence on the rationality of materialism has given way to a considered acceptance that the individual can experience and observe supernatural events. ✳

FIANT LVMINARIA IN FIRMAMENTO CELI

# TO CLIMB A TREE

*Becoming Rooted in Shenandoah*

**AMEI SHANK**

WHEN I WAS A COLLEGE STU-dent in New York City, I often daydreamed about climbing trees. It would happen like this: I would look up from my desk, my eyes dizzied from the itty-bitty textbook font they had been parsing for the past hour, and stare out the window. There wasn't much of a view—my window directly faced the brick dorm room across from mine—but there was a tree whose thick branches swept in and provided the only pop of variety in the rectangular scene. My imaginary self would climb out onto the fire escape, hop onto said branches, and make her way up.

Unfortunately, my real self never thought she had the physical agility or the time to climb trees. It was far more practical to climb preprofessional and academic ladders. My life was composed of studying, volunteer shifts, and hurried lunches on subway commutes that carried me from one extracurricular responsibility to another. I scheduled catching up with friends in whatever rectangular sliver of time Google Calendar told me I could spare. I wanted to become a doctor, and this was what people told me I had to do to get there. Family members lovingly remarked that I had my whole future ahead of me, and I wanted

nothing more than to skip ahead to it. To me, the present was about the future, and so it felt expendable. Year after year, I put my head down and went through the motions. Surely I would thank myself someday.

The coronavirus pandemic brought with it a sudden and sorely needed reality check. With the nationwide transition to remote classes, I said goodbye to my tree in the window when I moved out of my dorm room in the city and into my father's rural childhood home, where he was living at the time. It was a 250-year-old farmhouse in the heart of the Shenandoah Valley that had housed my family for eight generations, ever since my fifth great-grandfather purchased the land around the time of the Revolutionary War. Entering through its doors was like setting foot in an ancestral museum of sorts. "That's where Mom made soap out of lye," my father would reminisce, "and that table corner is where your Uncle Joe knocked out his front teeth during a game of tag."

When I first arrived in Virginia, the world felt like it had been flipped on its head. I had spent most of my life up to that point within a highly structured academic environment, striving for the top grades and most impressive accolades. Now all of a sudden, grading systems were pass/fail,

**I could already feel the pangs of regret and sadness that would overwhelm my older self upon realizing that there was little in her life to look back on. Delayed gratification was the name of the game I was playing, but I had only just grasped that time would run out one day.**

extracurricular activities ceased to exist, and free time was in gross abundance. For the first time in a long time, I was left to sit with my real self. The problem was I had no idea what to do with her.

Looking back on my undergraduate years, I came to the sobering realization that I could only remember a handful of moments. Everything else had coalesced into a singular haze of late nights at my desk. This terrified me. If I kept doing what I was doing, would my whole life be reduced to a similar haze of indistinguishable workdays? I could already feel the pangs of regret and sadness that would overwhelm my older self upon realizing that there was little in her life to look back on. Delayed gratification was the name of the game I was playing, but I had only just grasped that time would run out one day.

I wanted a life that was worth telling my future children about—one full of excitement, happiness, and meaning. But what made me happy? What mattered to me? Societal standards told me that someone with my background and credentials should be on the fast track to a good life, whatever that meant. Yet here I was, a soon-to-be college graduate, and I didn't know the answers to such basic questions. I had trained myself for so long to be a certain type of person that I found it extremely difficult to disentangle that person from who I really was.

Funnily enough, there was a tree just like the one in New York peeking into view through the window frame of my new room. This time, I decided to go outside and sit beneath it.

To say the valley was beautiful would be doing it a disservice. My new backyard was a vast tapestry of lush green pastures and sun-kissed rolling hills, punctuated by winding streams and lively family farms. When the sun set, the clouds were spun into pink cotton candy tufts.

My family's history was woven into this farmland even more deeply than into the farmhouse. For over two centuries, those 160 acres and the livestock that lived on the land had fed and sustained my ancestors. They were conservative Mennonites from Germany who immigrated to America in search of religious freedom and economic opportunity. The valley offered them the fertile land they needed to cultivate their family and their faith. When their time came, many chose to be buried in the family cemetery and return to the soil that had nourished them. The cemetery plot still sits in its own idyllic pocket on the farm, perched on top of a hill overlooking the Blue Ridge Mountains. The valley continues to be home to a large Mennonite community that includes many of my family members. Although most of them have broken away from some of the community's more traditional practices, their faith remains their foremost guiding force in life. When I was growing up, my father occasionally shared accounts of his upbringing on the farm and in the Mennonite church, but I never thought much about these parts of my heritage until the farm started to feel like home.

I began taking walks regularly. To tread along the same paths my predecessors once did recentered me in a way I didn't expect. Their decades of labor on this very land made my existence possible, and for that, I felt an immense gratitude. I had always known factually where I came from, but it felt completely different to internalize it and conceptualize myself as being part of a bigger legacy. Occasionally, I would run into some relatives who lived on the other side of the farm. They were always on an adventure: they swam in streams in the forest, played with wild animals, and hurtled down the hills in their ATVs. There was a certain trust they had in the land that I marveled at; in situations where I would be wary of getting lost or hurt, they were unafraid and full of life.

Being in their company gradually broadened my appreciation for the world around me. My

*Olivia Pendergast*

life before the pandemic had wound my thoughts into tight, rigid coils, but being in this space was slowly releasing the tension. My mind was freed to wander and reflect in ways that it hadn't since I was younger. Before I knew it, I was operating large farm equipment, jumping on top of hay bales, planting trees, and befriending a group of stray cats that lived on the farm. I did actually try to climb a tree, though I didn't get far. These are all simple things, but they brought me a new sense of peace that I didn't want to let go of. To place your faith in the earth upon which you walk is to allow your eyes to look to the world above. The running joke in the family was that the city girl had been converted into a farmhand.

Everyone in the community treated one another with the same respect and trust they gave the land. One of the first times I went for a walk, several passersby honked and greeted me from the road as they drove past the house. Initially, this puzzled me—the parallel situation in Manhattan would have been interpreted as peculiar and potentially unnerving. In reality, these people were continuing to look out for their neighbors even during a time of unprecedented social isolation.

Why did I see a simple gesture of kindness with such skepticism? Sure, there were natural cultural differences, but it felt bigger than that. Kindness was enacted for kindness's sake. It really was that simple. Everyone understood compassion and peacemaking through the word of God and spent their days spreading both.

Whenever my father ate at a restaurant by himself, his bill was more often than not picked up by unidentified strangers. He could have taken insult from the possibility that these people pitied him, but instead, he was grateful.

# The Shenandoah Valley taught me beauty, compassion, faith, and gratitude for life. It slowed me down until my real and imaginary selves could collapse into one whole person.

A family friend paid for hotel rooms and offered transport to those without a home on especially cold nights. He could have assumed the worst of these individuals and passed them by, but he did not. A neighbor and devoted father mowed a heart the size of a baseball diamond on the side of the road every few days to memorialize his love for his family. People did not concern themselves with questioning others' motives or backgrounds or anything of the sort. Instead, it was the default to assume good and true intentions. In my experience, it was the other way around in most places. However, being on the receiving end of this kindness showed me that that did not have to be the case. To have strangers go out of their way to help me made me want to be better for them and others.

In the Mennonite faith, simplicity is a companion to compassion. Theirs is a world where prestige, social status, and material wealth hold little importance. They believe that God created humans to better the world and the lives of one another. How each person carries this out depends on the strengths and gifts they are endowed with. If recognition and abundance are byproducts of the journey, then that is fine, but they should not be ends themselves. This makes for a life less crowded by these pursuits, with greater room for things more fundamentally human—namely family, faith, and self-reflection—things I had historically pushed to the side. To see that there was a world where your achievements were peripheral to who you were lifted an enormous weight off my shoulders. The members of this community lived their lives in ways that pushed against nearly every aspect of how I was used to living, and yet I saw that they were content. Their contentment came, in some cases, because they seemed to possess answers to questions I did not and, in other cases, because they seemed committed to asking deeper questions even when answers did not present themselves.

That includes how to think about death. One perfectly normal afternoon, my uncle passed away from a sudden heart attack. It happened right before my father and I were about to meet him for one of our weekly picnics. To me, death was too-big funeral halls filled with more tears and regrets than people. Death was head-splitting grief that pulled families apart. It was the greatest enemy to us all.

But what if it didn't have to be? Here, to my surprise, death was a complicated ally. It still imposed a deep sadness and pain, but it was not malicious. I remember it was especially beautiful and sunny on the day of my uncle's funeral. This felt odd at first—anything pleasant or positive seemed out of place, wrong even. Yet, when I looked around, I saw attendees fondly reminiscing and embracing each other. Tears were shed, but they were not bred from anger or hopelessness. Instead, there was a palpable air of acceptance. Though my uncle was no longer with us, he would be looked after in God's capable hands, and that was a blessing. Even under the tragic circumstances, the gathering felt like a celebration of life rather than a solemn farewell. It was healing. Suddenly, I was grateful for the sunshine. Uncle Dale certainly deserved it.

The funeral brought me back to my days volunteering at a hospital in New York. During that time, I once spent an afternoon with a man who was very near the end of his life. I recalled his bright blue eyes, which looked as though the light that once shone in them had been extinguished. With no loved ones to visit him, he had only me to accompany him in his final hours. Though I was a complete stranger, he treated me like a close confidant in our short time together. "You know, I dedicated my life to my career. I made a lot of money and was very successful," he said with a hollow sigh. He paused for a while before he weakly muttered, "Now I'm dying and I'm all alone."

Up until then, I had actively avoided thinking about mortality, especially my own. Like in a children's game of hot potato, I tossed the thought away as soon as it came to me. That day, however, I sat with it out of respect for the man, despite my discomfort. For a while, his voice echoed in my mind, prompting me to pause and reflect on my life. Looking back, I believe he was trying to caution me. I think he saw a young girl just starting out and was doing his best to show her what mattered in the end. Nevertheless, my memory of the man, along with any wisdom he had tried to pass down to me, eventually faded.

Uncle Dale always used to urge me to step away from my desk and go outside, though I usually dismissed him. It was only after he passed that I was transported back to that patient's bedside and I began to understand the weight of both of their words. The ideas they expressed were not new to me. After all, we have all been surrounded by advice from older generations as well as flurries of "carpe diem," "you only live once," "stop and smell the roses," and the like for millennia. Despite this, many of us don't fully absorb the meaning of these sentiments until we approach the end of our own lives. Realizing this compelled something in me to push against this cycle. Although I had lived a life of busyness up till that point, I could heed the advice of the many before me to make the most of the time ahead.

The Shenandoah Valley taught me beauty, compassion, faith, and gratitude for life. It slowed me down until my real and imaginary selves could collapse into one whole person instead of existing separately. The same girl who wanted to become a doctor could also scale the branches of the walnut tree outside her room. Although I still had a lifetime's worth of things to learn, I was beginning to understand myself. What made me happy? A day out in the sun, long chats with a friend, a piping hot bowl of chili, surprising someone with a thoughtful gift. What mattered to me? Having a happy family, making memories on adventures, and spending my days bettering the lives of others. I believe seeking the answers to these questions, and subsequently centering our lives around what we find, is the true and most essential climb we should embark on. Whether that leads to a tree, to a canvas, or back to school, the older versions of ourselves will surely look back and smile.

*Olivia Pendergast*

*Olivia Pendergast*

Today, I am a student again. This time, I live in Silicon Valley, a place where life moves at the breakneck speed of the most advanced technologies. I study at an institution whose name is synonymous with prestige, where distinctions and h-indices are social currencies. The rat race goes on, and I'd be lying if I said I didn't sometimes still run it.

Just the other day, I felt a jolt of panic after overhearing a classmate talk about the numerous research projects they were working on. It was almost a knee-jerk reaction to reach for my laptop and scroll through projects that I could join. Unlike in college, I now catch myself in these moments. I recognize that these kinds of actions are coming from a place of insecurity and comparison, not of true interest. I'm in medical school to become the kind of doctor and person who can touch the hearts of those I will care for one day. Because of that, I try my best to spend my days doing things that I genuinely care about. That also means turning down a lot of opportunities. Coming to terms with this trade-off is not easy, but I've found that going into things with a "why" makes even the most challenging and uncomfortable situations feel worthwhile.

To be honest, it has been incredibly difficult to maintain this mindset. Sometimes it feels like everything around me is pushing me to revert to my old habits. The modern agenda allows increasingly less time for pursuits that aren't overtly productive. More often than not, it's the opportunities I'm not interested in that seem like they'll get me further, faster.

Whenever I start to feel lost, I think about the drivers who waved at me from the road, the community members who inspired me with their unwavering faith, and the man with the blue eyes. I've gone back to church for the first time in over a decade. I contemplate my older self and how she will die one day. Maybe we all have our own tree in the window—something that calls to who we really are inside but gets sidelined by tasks immediately in front of us. Maybe if we traded our devices for some rope and boosted each other up, we could all make it up in our own time. The view, I'm sure, is extraordinary. I'll meet you there. ✳

# APPROACHING THE TEMPLE

LINDA
HOFFMAN
KIMBALL

I confess You elude me a bit
In the signs others see:
In the clothing-just-so,
In the particulars of gesture,
In the murmurations
Both – they say – ancient
And the clearly new.
It is a code immune
to my gentle explorations.
But I sense You in the
Hands held,
In the Godly cascade
Of names
Chanted
through all time,
spilling through laced fingers,
over altars, beyond slippers,
joining the holy flow
toward the eternal,
fruitful Tree.

# GOD OF OUR CHILDREN

**MIKAYLA ORTON THATCHER
& NATHAN THATCHER**

God of our chil - dren, help us make a home for them—
God of the need - y, show us how to tru - ly give
God of the out - cast, par - don us where we have failed.

Ha - vens of safe - ty to learn and to grow.
Our hearts and sub - stance, so all may be filled.
Help us make space here for all to be - long.

God of our el - ders, teach us how to love through
God of the help - less, we will, with Your aid, build
God of cre - a - tion, we strive to be one, by

ag - ing and grief toward chang - es yet un - known.
plac - es that wel - come and ne - ver for - bid.
prac - tic - ing love that we've learned from Your Son.

Words: Mikayla Orton Thatcher (b. 1991)
Music: Nathan Thatcher (b. 1989)

To listen to a recording of this hymn, visit
wayfaremagazine.org/p/god-of-our-children.

# WHAT THE PROPHET SAW

*Scripture as an Artistic Endeavor*

**TYLER JOHNSON**

IN MY EXPERIENCE, WHAT WE look for influences what we are likely to find, and that is nowhere more true than in the context of scripture study. If you are like me, perhaps you have turned to scripture with the expectation of finding an answer to a question, or finding peace during tribulation. And those are understandable and worthy aims. Still, thinking about what we hope scripture will offer us begs some fundamental questions: What are scriptures, exactly, and how do we use them as we seek to connect with God?

I can see how my expectations about scripture change depending on my circumstances and mindset. At times I have found them useful as a sort of recipe book that teaches me how to follow a set of practices that will bring me closer to God. Other times I have read scripture as an inspirational guide that, in a holistic manner, helps me design and build my own life as a disciple. These modes of reading scripture share the common idea that scripture is intended to communicate immutable truths, and that the role of the prophets who penned them is to transcribe such truths to the best of their abilities. Accordingly, the ideal prophet would function as a transparent intermediary: God utters the words, so to speak, and the job of the prophet is simply to write them down. One friend of mine summarized this theory of scripture by saying that scripture (and general conference talks) are like "text messages from God."

As appealing as this conception of scripture might be, further reflection—and my own limited experience with the ineffable—suggests that such a view might be misleading, or at least incomplete. Elements of our theology and history indicate that we have other ways to understand prophets and their words as found in scripture. I believe we need to grapple with the possibility that the creation and function of scripture do not work only as a divine communication transmission. In fact, understanding scripture only as "text messages from God" may needlessly limit the truths we glean from scripture precisely because that view limits the ways in which we can understand divine truth. In this essay, then, I want to ask: how else might we describe scripture, and what does it mean for our personal devotional practices?

As I think along these lines, I am brought to think about one of my favorite paintings, *Wanderer Above the Sea of Fog*, by Caspar David Friedrich.

This painting is considered one of the masterpieces of the German Romantic era, the

**The figure in the painting, though depicted in the foreground, remains dwarfed by the landscape he is beholding—he is not a titan, not a colossus, but a man faced with an overwhelming scene.**

quintessential *Rückenfigur* painting. This style of painting depicts its primary subject from the back, robbing us of the opportunity to see the figure's face and thus focusing us on what the figure is experiencing. In the case of this painting, it brings our sight toward the landscape upon which the central figure gazes, sometimes seen as representing "the sublime."

I love this painting as a metaphor for the prophetic project for multiple reasons. The first is that the painting pulls us *away* from the prophet himself and *toward* that to which the prophets point us—the sublime in the painting, Jesus Christ in our theology. Beyond that, the painting reminds me that prophets, too, are humans just like we are. The figure in the painting, though depicted in the foreground, remains dwarfed by the landscape he is beholding—he is not a titan, not a colossus, but a man faced with an overwhelming scene.

But the most important truth this painting suggests to me concerns what a prophet is and does, especially in relation to how we think about scripture. To me, the most powerful idea the painting conveys comes when I think about this question: "What would it be like if this man came back to me—assuming I had never looked upon the scene he is seeing and have never glimpsed this painting—and tried to explain to me what that landscape was like?"

Words would fail him.

They would not fail because he is not eloquent—Neal A. Maxwell and Jeffrey R. Holland, for example, are both quite eloquent, as are Alma, Paul, Isaiah, and Benjamin (and, for that matter, as are Kate Holbrook, Eliza R. Snow, and Melissa Inouye)—but rather because words simply cannot convey the full force and beauty of a scene

like the one this man confronts. In some cases, this is a question of ineloquence (Moses's "I am slow of speech, and of a slow tongue," Exod. 4:10), but in other cases it is a testament to *the categorical inadequacy of words to convey divine truth.*

What strikes me about this is that *prophets are deeply conscious of—and self-conscious about—this inadequacy.* Indeed, their concerns about this limitation pervade scripture. I have already mentioned Moses. Likewise, it was Joseph Smith—that endless fount of revelations of every stripe—who lamented that English was a "little narrow prison almost as it were totel [*sic*] darkness of paper pen and ink and a crooked broken scattered and imperfect language."[1]

Similarly, this theme asserts itself insistently from the beginning to the end of the Book of Mormon. Nephi laments in his last eponymous chapter, "I, Nephi, cannot write all the things which were taught among my people; neither am I mighty in writing" (1 Ne. 33:1). And Moroni, who thought he was writing the compendium's benediction and had almost closed (as he supposed) the entire record, intoned this stunning epigraph memorializing the limitations of both prophets and language: "Condemn me not because of mine imperfection, neither my father, because of his imperfection, neither them who have written before him; but rather give thanks unto God that he hath made manifest unto you our imperfections, that ye may learn to be more wise than we have been" (Mormon 9:31).

In other words, if I can add a bit of nonscriptural elaboration (including ideas found elsewhere in that same chapter), Moroni is saying, "God, I recognize that this record can never fully convey the weight of these ideas, but please let these imperfect words carry the beauty of the grace of Jesus to the hearts of those who will read them, and let those readers turn to Christ, who will bring to them the fully transcendent life these words never can."

In this verse, I see Moroni envisioning himself (as it were) as the faceless figure in *Wanderer Above the Sea of Fog.* He gazes out on the stunning expanse depicted in that painting—only infinite and even more beautiful—and then turns to God in desperation, asking, in effect, "How on earth

*Caspar David Friedrich*

am I ever supposed to convey even the thousandth part of that to other people by writing little squiggles on metal plates, never mind that those squiggles will then require multiple translations across time, culture, language, and space?"

The idea makes reason stare.

Reading Moroni's words in this way, the prophetic and scriptural project moves beyond the idea of a person perfectly transmitting language that awaits in some heavenly vault. Such a conception, after all, could suggest something like prophetic perfection, implying that the prophet acts as divine medium for hallowed words, which further suggests that the words themselves almost require their own worship. Rather, scripture becomes something like a prophet's artistic endeavor (even if most prophets do not see themselves as artists). I come to see a prophet as a person who is encountering the sacred and the ineffable in a visceral, personal, and immediate fashion and who is now tasked with communicating with us—in whatever way possible—the reality of that experience, and who will then invite us to have that experience for ourselves.

Let us look at Alma 5. This chapter can be read in more than one mode. We can read it as a set of best practices that leads us to happiness (it is often described as an "interview" we might have with ourselves). We can be inspired by its description of a disciple's life. Or we can read it as an artistic expression of Alma's transcendent experience with the power of the Atonement of Jesus Christ and the overwhelming moral suasion of that love. I don't mean to suggest that one mode of reading this chapter is the "best," "highest," or "right" way. I value the insights I have gained from this chapter by reading in multiple modes.

Still, I did not feel like I really began to grasp what Alma might be getting at until I began to think of him as the faceless wanderer from the painting. Only, in this case, I believe he comes to us in that mode with a very specific message.

We have to remember that Alma spends his ministry haunted by the prospect of the hell he believed was yawning to swallow him up if he had not repented. Or, rather, the hell whose flames already arose to lick him when he realized the harm he had done during his wanton

**I come to see a prophet as a person who is encountering the sacred and the ineffable in a visceral, personal, and immediate fashion and who is now tasked with communicating with us—in whatever way possible—the reality of that experience, and who will then invite us to have that experience for ourselves.**

years. This is all to say: Alma 36 makes it clear, in Alma's stunning poetry, that his central ministerial concern was to discover a language that could come close to conveying the full beauty, splendor, majesty, and transformative power of the divine love, saving grace, and Atonement of Jesus Christ.

Understood in this way, Alma's sermon in chapter 5 becomes an attempt over and over and over again to convey what he clearly knows he cannot fully or adequately convey. He begins the chapter by describing the physical deliverance of the people from King Noah and then analogizes this to the spiritual deliverance all must seek at the hands of Jesus. As he reminds his listeners, "Were the bands of death broken, and the chains of hell which encircled them about, were they loosed? I say unto you, Yea, they were loosed, and their souls did expand, and they did sing redeeming love. And I say unto you that they are saved" (Alma 5:9).

This idea of deliverance and salvation will be the theme of the rest of the sermon—everything he says is his faltering attempt to convey a beauty whose full grandeur compels but forever eludes him. This is Alma staring out into the sublime— that faceless wanderer, again—and then looking inside himself and seeing there the beauty that has arisen from ashes. This is Alma saying, "I have seen salvation, and I am going to try—but fail—to use this sermon to tell you what it is like."

But what touches me so deeply is that, read in this way, Alma's sermon is nearly childlike in its earnest and enthusiastic attempt to convey something he does not have the words to communicate, like a five-year-old left spitting and sputtering as she tries to explain a wonderful new taste or sensation. Alma tosses out words and comparisons and analogies at such a furious pace, and with such reckless literary abandon, it's almost hard to keep up. Read this way, the sermon is not only a doctrinal treatise but also the portrait of a poet wrestling mightily with the universe's most sublime idea—the love of God. This chapter becomes poignant precisely because of Alma's rhetorical inadequacy. He never succeeds in his poetic endeavor, but gosh doesn't he *just keep trying*.

Alma asks, implicitly: What is it like to be rescued by Jesus?

The rest of his chapter is the answer:

It's like being delivered from a wicked king!

No, wait, it's like having manacles snapped in two!

No, wait, it's like being born a second time!

No, wait, it's like being given a second heart!

No, wait, it's like being cleansed when you were dirty!

No, wait, it's like learning to sing a new and transcendent song!

And on and on the list goes.

But the point in all this is not any single analogy, but rather the cumulative effect of all the analogies and the very fact that even all of them together still fall short. Like the sublime landscape in the painting, the entire point is how wholly inadequate is a painting, much less any person's attempt to describe a painting, to convey the full beauty and splendor of the love of God.

Seen in this way, the entire scriptural and prophetic project, in at least one sense, becomes an attempt by those who have been transformed by the alchemy of divine love to use scattered, broken, and imperfect words to invite all of us to experience with personal immediacy the gathered, whole, and perfect love of Jesus. ✳

1.   Joseph Smith to William W. Phelps, November 27, 1832, p. 4, Joseph Smith Papers.

# EVE'S KNOWLEDGE REVEALED IN DREAMS

EMILY
UPDEGRAFF

She sleeps hidden from petal-footed
carnivores stealthing through pre-dawn dew,
their ears tuned to weakness. Her eyes open
to vernal light and she turns to the problem
of living–what to do about fire, food,
and the children's nakedness. No wonder
that the first thing our first parents received
was clothing. Imagine how they lived.
Hunger, blisters, bites from creeping things,
muscles sheared to make the soil give way.
And with each birth our mother ceded
power for the privilege of sitting still
long enough to feed her baby, her womb
cramping and her world contracting, even
as inward spheres multiply. While she sleeps,
muscle fibers heal themselves, synapses
thicken, and the coiled emotions of last
night's conflict unwind. Her dreams of flight
are blanked out by the light of the morning.
What remains is insight: how to stop grain
from molding, how to tie the child so he
feels light on her back, how to wrap a wound
in lamb's ear and heal it.

# REDEEMING THE DEAD

*The Power & Potential of Temple Worship*

PETER MUGEMANCURO

I ATTENDED A TEMPLE ENDOW-
ment session for the first time as a sullen
eighteen-year-old, grudgingly preparing for
my mission to Chicago. I have always been very
aware of my personal imperfections; the white,
soaring walls of the LA temple felt forbidding
and even uninviting that day as I walked inside.
As I waited for the ceremony to start, I wondered,
*Should I even be here?* I'd spent the last six months
trying to figure out how I could leave the Church
without kicking up too much fuss, and yet here
I was on the verge of making commitments to
God that in my mind I'd have no choice but to
try and keep for the rest of my life. The cognitive
dissonance made me feel punishingly out of place.
The unfamiliar wording and symbolism of the
endowment session only heightened my impos-
tor syndrome. As I was invited to keep the law of
chastity, I was uncomfortably reminded of my
bisexuality. My hand went up in grim assent even
as I thought, *This could get me in serious trouble
later.* I came to the end of the ceremony confused,
a little stunned, and almost entirely uncompre-
hending. If I was supposed to have seen angels or
had visions, I had utterly failed. I felt the Spirit a
little, but only around the edges.

I went to the temple again near the end of
my mission in Chicago. The missionaries in my
cohort had come out six months before the start
of the coronavirus pandemic; quite a few of us
went home early, and those who remained had
served in circumstances that we never would
have bargained for. Entering the Chicago temple
that day, I felt a profound sense of wholeness. For
Latter-day Saints, the temple is where we're supposed to experience what it's like to be in God's
presence. I was there with some of my closest
friends. We'd served together, laughed together,
and suffered together. We probably wouldn't
ever all be in the same place again. This time, the
endowment ceremony washed over me in waves
of grateful appreciation. Somehow it seemed
much more familiar; once-confusing symbols and
words held a far richer significance. Entering the
celestial room of the temple was everything I'd
ever imagined it would or could be; it felt like I
was entering the presence of God. When the time
came to leave, I didn't want to go. My soul was
abundantly satisfied. I didn't see angels or have
visions, but I felt God loved me to the point
where it overwhelmed my senses. The Spirit was
so intense that I cannot put it into words.

I don't share these experiences in this order to suggest some sort of nice, linear pathway from doubt to faith—since I've come home from my mission, my temple worship has continued to both inspire and challenge me. I share them because they nicely highlight one of the Church's unspoken fault lines: the gulf between those who feel comfortable attending the temple and those who do not. Holding a current temple recommend sometimes feels like the Latter-day Saint equivalent of an American Express Gold Card, offering access to all the spiritual (and social) benefits of Church membership. By contrast, not holding one (or not living the Church's moral standards with sufficient rigor to attend) might feel like a shabby, second-tier alternative, a sort of Mormonism-lite. While I personally choose to hold a current recommend and do my best to live the associated standards, some friends whom I deeply care about have found that they don't feel comfortable playing word games in ecclesiastical interviews when their genuine love for the Savior and his gospel doesn't quite stretch to an uncritical embrace of his restored Church. As a Black,

*Elise Wehle*

queer, and nevertheless fully active member of the Church, I have learned through abundant personal experience that those two feelings are not necessarily the same thing.

This all being said, my personal experience also tells me that attending the temple is much, much more than a sort of spiritual Disneyland fast pass. I find genuine power there, much more so because of the effort required to align my life with the standards for attendance. The temple is the place where I most strongly feel that God cares about the things that matter to me—even if it's a difficult exam or a passing relationship worry. My worship there is a compelling source of personal light and truth, and I am not ashamed when I say that it's literally the house of God.

How can both of these things be true? How can the temple simultaneously be a place of stinging alienation and ineffable spiritual uplift? More to the point, how might we as disciples mentally separate the spiritual gifts available in the temple from the exhausting rat race of performative righteousness that all too often stokes the alienation in the first place? For me, the answers that resonate lie in attempting to see Jesus and engage with his gospel more intentionally.

In Doctrine and Covenants section 70, the Lord put Joseph Smith, Oliver Cowdery, and others in charge of publishing the revelations that the Church had received through Joseph up to that point. In verses 2 and 3, the Lord says, "I, the Lord, have appointed them, and ordained them to be stewards over the revelations and commandments which I have given . . . and an account of this stewardship will I require of them in the day of judgment" (D&C 70:2–3). This idea of stewardship over spiritual things (as opposed to merely temporal ones) also shows up in the New Testament: in 1 Corinthians 4, Paul writes, "Let a man so account of us, as of the ministers of Christ, and stewards of the mysteries of God" (1 Cor 4:1).

For me, the concept of spiritual stewardship suggests at least two things: first, it would be wrong to claim ownership over the spiritual gifts we've been given, either individually or collectively; and second, all of us are personally responsible to God for how we use the spiritual tools we have access to. Theologically speaking, none of us—not even the Church—owns the spiritual blessings of the temple. Yes, the Church pours the concrete and pays the electrical bills, but we make the promises and experience (or not) the spiritual fruits of living them. Choosing to serve in the temple and live the covenants is far less about our standing in the Church than it is about speaking with and worshiping God. Of course, Church leaders have been saying this consistently for years; the difficulty is that from a cultural perspective it's unclear if we fully believe them.

So what are our spiritual responsibilities as stewards of the covenants we make? For me, regular temple attendance immediately comes to mind. I personally struggle to fit it into my schedule as often as I say I'd like; there are many worthwhile (and less worthwhile) things competing for my time and attention. I'll go "when I need answers" or when I feel prompted to do so, but these instances are by definition both unscheduled and somewhat infrequent. Of course, we might conceive of more expansive spiritual responsibilities than just attendance: for instance, how should our individual stewardship of the temple influence our defining, daily interactions with spouses, children, and parents? How might they help us see even the most difficult people in our lives as children of God with infinite potential for giving and receiving divine love? If the temple is really as powerful as we say it is—if it is a place where God resides—our worship there ought to have transformative effects on our families, communities, and even the world. In a very literal sense, it ought to help us build Zion.

I first experienced the universal, all-inclusive potential of our temple worship a few years ago when I was one of the Latter-day Saint college students selected to participate in the Amos C. Brown fellowship program in Ghana. The Church partnered with the NAACP to make the trip in an attempt to build bridges of understanding, open lines of communication between people at all levels of the two organizations, and reckon with America's legacy of racism and discrimination. Predictably, it was impossible to be in that space without pointed and valid questions about our church's own history of racism and discrimination; there were many hard conversations as we joined with our college-age peers in the NAACP in trying to reckon with the trip's vexing and complicated context.

Our itinerary didn't make the experience any easier: on the second-to-last day of the trip we visited one of the slave castles in Cape Coast.

## The intense darkness of the place far surpassed the physical dimness of the dungeon: it was the closest thing to pure evil I think I've experienced. I felt depressed, broken, and exhausted.

The whitewashed walls shone in the sun, but the rusting cannon facing seaward spoke to the fort's original purpose. Down in the bowels of the structure, below ground level and with only one remote window for light, we saw the pits where up to a thousand people at a time were kept in suffocating conditions for weeks before being loaded onto slave ships. It was explained to us that slavers sought to eradicate all traces of individual identity—whether relational, tribal, or cultural—by separating newly enslaved people from their families and treating them worse than animals. Since my dad came to the US from Rwanda and I don't have enslaved ancestors, I wasn't mentally prepared for the visceral, awful discomfort that enshrouded me. The intense darkness of the place far surpassed the physical dimness of the dungeon: it was the closest thing to pure evil I think I've experienced. I felt depressed, broken, and exhausted.

The next day, our last in Ghana, our schedule was open in the morning, and the Latter-day Saint students had the opportunity to go to the Accra temple for a few hours. As we began performing baptisms for the dead, I noticed that the names on the ordinance cards were all Congolese. I was struck by the unexpected but powerful parallelism. The previous day, we'd been in a place where African identity was ripped away and African families were torn apart; now, we were performing ordinances that treated the ancestors of living African Church members with dignity

> ## We can intentionally fill our lives with his love, sharing it with others along the way until one day we step back into his presence and find ourselves truly, perfectly, and eternally at home.

and reverence, symbolically honoring their lives and giving them a way to be united with their families forever.

In our theology, performing temple ordinances for the dead does not force them to become part of our church. Rather, it gives them the choice to posthumously accept the gospel of Jesus Christ and—we believe—gain access to the possibility of eternal life with those they love. It is a mark of honor and respect. My time performing these ordinances in the Accra temple became far more for me than a matter of personal faith practice—the hour or so I spent there morphed into a serious and important opportunity to participate in God's work, extending justice and mercy further into a world that desperately needed it. We often speak in the Church of blessing the whole human family with our temple and missionary work, but never before in my life had I so clearly seen what that process might look like.

If our temple worship gives us unique opportunities to bless the world, it is uniquely our responsibility to put them to use. The ceremonies we perform there are not to be found in any other Christian tradition, and even if they were, no other faith tradition can speak our theological

and cultural language quite like we can. The Book of Mormon teaches that God "speaketh unto men according to their language" and that he "doth grant unto all nations . . . to teach his word, yea, in wisdom, all that he seeth fit that they should have" (2 Ne 31:4; Alma 29:8). These scriptures suggest to me a God who is acutely sensitive to the cultural and spiritual diversity of his children, sending forth divine light in numerous ways; however, they also suggest to me a God whose desire to bless us is contingent on our willingness to understand and engage with the spiritual truth available to us. If the temple really is what it claims to be, we as Latter-day Saints have inherited a deep, undeserved, and priceless vessel of heavenly light. In that case, what we choose to do with it is genuinely important.

While I hope I've made the case that the temple can have symbolic and spiritual meaning far outside our Latter-day Saint tradition, I still haven't addressed its potential as a source of alienation for those inside it. What does our spiritual stewardship have to say about this? Several thoughts come to mind.

Given what the temple offers, it seems reasonable that the question of who gets to participate in the ordinances is something for which our entire church will ultimately be held accountable to God. I have often reflected on the fact that if I'd been born forty years sooner, I wouldn't have had access to the temple for reasons beyond my control. More vexingly, it wouldn't surprise me if in the future I lose the access I currently have due to my desire for human connections of the sort that the Church does not recognize. Although it might seem strange, neither of these things leads me to question the temple's underlying legitimacy. Explaining why not could be an essay of its own, but the shortest reason I could give is that I've had enough profound temple experiences to firmly believe that the divine power I experience there is real. It influences my life in ways that both sanctify and enhance my self-conception as a child of God. The pain that I have felt and may yet feel because of these difficult questions is pain that I believe Jesus has already suffered on my behalf. Choosing to mentally invalidate

*Elise Wehle*

or ignore the profound spiritual experiences I've had wouldn't help me to face the apparent contradictions I live in with any greater equanimity; paradoxically, fully embracing my spiritual heritage has given me the ability to think productively about questions that would otherwise be far too difficult for me.

On a more general level, it is perhaps unwise for us to let ourselves conceive of the temple doors as being meant to keep people *out*. Just as we might go to a grocery store to pick up food for someone who is housebound, we could probably get better at "translating" the light and truth we can receive through temple worship into the lives of everyone around us—members and nonmembers alike—who cannot at the moment access it for themselves. If the temple gives us added strength to cope with our individual challenges, our baptismal covenants remind us that at least a part of that strength ought to go towards bearing the burdens of others. Stewardship is not ownership. Since we do not own the temple, thinking of its power purely in terms of our own spiritual

health (or worse, as part of one of our seemingly unending righteousness checklists) is misguided and profoundly stifling.

Jesus memorably taught, "Men [do not] light a candle and put it under a bushel, but on a candlestick; and it giveth light unto all that are in the house" (Mt 5:15). For us as Latter-day Saints, the temple is perhaps the most salient mechanism for dispensing the light that can come into our lives through the teachings of Jesus. In a world that seems more chaotic and confusing each day, our quiet, consistent ability to project that kind of light into our families and communities is increasingly important. Whether or not we hold a temple recommend—whether or not we fully feel as though we belong in our wards or in the Church—we can all do more to cultivate our relationship with Jesus through the indescribable spiritual gifts he has given us. We can intentionally fill our lives with his love, sharing it with others along the way until one day we step back into his presence and find ourselves truly, perfectly, and eternally at home. ✴

# HEAVEN'S LAUGHTER

WILLIAM
MORRIS

WHY DO SO MANY AUTHORS, FILM-makers, and artists seem to suspect that heaven is boring? I wonder if it's because we can't seem to conceive of a perfection that's not, in some sense, totalitarian—all smoothed out by God's all-encompassing will.

Even in positive portrayals,[1] heaven is—at best—innocuous, bureaucratic, and oblivious to the complexity and actual concerns of humanity.

> ## How do you tell a joke in the language of heaven? Jokes require disjunctures and slippages of meaning— the ability to surprise.

Behind the idealized exterior, heaven has a certain emptiness. Its inhabitants are still going through the motions, but it's not clear if anything inside is really driving them.

Hell in fiction, meanwhile, is terrible, but at least it seems interesting precisely because it's not perfect. A rebellious, earth-bound Lucifer is simply a more compelling character than a distant, perfect God the Father.

I'm a writer and also a believer. To be specific: I believe in heaven, art, humor, the agency of humanity, and the persistence of individual being.

None of this is normally a problem. These elements have been fertile ground for exploration in both my writing and daily and religious life. But lately I've been thinking about them all together as a set and have discovered that I'm unsure how they ultimately fit together. If we're talking about a heaven filled with perfect beings working in line with God's will, what is comedy about? Do perfect people crack jokes?

The possibility of heavenly laughter is, for me, an important question. So much of heaven

*Brian T. Kershisnik*

depends on how we understand the nature of God, evil, agency, and the like. Like Joseph Smith, I want to cram as much humanity and embodiment as possible into our heaven. I don't necessarily expect a heaven that is perfectly frictionless. I hope for a heaven where we can laugh.

How do you tell a joke in the language of heaven?

Jokes require disjunctures and slippages of meaning—the ability to surprise. It seems to me that humor requires difference and change, so a laughing heaven must be a place where those things are possible.

I believe in a heaven that changes. I believe in a heaven where perfection doesn't erase difference, personal history, and personality. Perfection

is what is perfect for that individual at that time and place. Perfect as a mode rather than a state. A perfection that is perfect enough to be malleable. And a changeable perfection leaves room for surprise, for delight, for laughter.

The very fact of humor affirms for me that our individuality of being and experience matters and persists into eternity. Because what's more hilarious, but also terrifying, than the belief that this existence (and the one before it and the one that comes after) actually, ultimately matters?

At the same time, that every aspect of our existence and experience matters is also comforting: there's this plan where divine Creators love their children and want what's best for them, which is that they grow and learn and desire to return to heaven and interact with them as parents and children do (in our more enlightened moments) here on earth.

And when we do arrive there, we're all connected together, hanging out in heaven, helping our Heavenly Parents with further acts of creation, meeting together, telling stories, cracking jokes—the full, rich, beautiful, human sound of laughter ringing into the eternities. ✳

*This short essay is an excerpt from a longer one that can be found at wayfaremagazine.org.*

1.   Such as in the ABC sitcom *The Good Place*.

# SUBTLE GRACE

*In Praise of Simple Blessings*

**MATTHEW WICKMAN**

EADER, MY NAME IS MATT, and I . . . I'm a recovering mirac-o-holic. I relish stories of God's miraculous intervention in matters of health, faith, love, opportunity, and more. I especially love these stories when they are my own. Like many of us, I have a few. And like virtually all of us, I would like more. But therein lies the problem. It's not a problem with the miracles, it's with the wanting. The expectation, the waiting. The worrying, the disappointment. For some of us, the disillusionment.

Inverting the famous lines from Cassius in Shakespeare's *Julius Caesar*, perhaps the fault lies not in ourselves but in our stars—in our culture—if we are spiritual underlings. As a backdrop, let me share a story that forms a parallel case. Years ago, in the shady chill of a November morning, I listened to my dad speak at an outdoor Veteran's Day ceremony at BYU. His subject, unsurprisingly, was patriotism. But he barbed his remarks by contrasting patriotism with a culture of heroism that denigrates it. These days, he said, we fetishize heroes: everyone wants to be a hero, and we inflate everyday figures—parents, public servants, sports figures—into heroes. Nothing against heroes, he insisted. He told a story of one

he'd known in Vietnam, a soldier who jumped onto a grenade and spared the lives of others in his patrol at the expense of his own. But when we obsess over heroism, he remarked, we overlook patriotism. In distracting ourselves with grandiose narratives, we neglect the honor bound up in simple, sometimes difficult acts of duty and fail to heed the humbler rhythms of our responsibility as citizens.

This contrast often comes to mind when I perceive traces of a culture of miracles in our religious communities. The operative word here is culture, derived from cultivation, bearing implications for how we learn to see, and shape, our relationship with the divine. I'm not referring to those remarkable experiences when God seems to intervene in people's lives in unimaginable and instantly transformative ways. Rather, I'm thinking of exaggerated cases that reduce the miraculous to the commonplace: overheated youth leaders equating simple testimony with a rending of the heavens, or young missionaries seeking a constant infusion of the "incredible" to justify and partly redeem the weighty toll of their daily grind. I'm thinking too of the kind of experience I had several years ago during a ward conference meeting when a stake officer gasped

## While miracles take myriad forms, blessings are exponentially more diverse and abundant.

"Miracle!"—startling the room—in response to my bishop's story of how neighborly befriending by our ward Relief Society had brought a long-time, less-active member back to church.

Faith that precedes a miracle is one thing. The social longing that craves Instagrammable memes of God's favor is something else. We can't help it: we're creatures of an Age of Spectacle. We love it when our religious experience feels as massive as a Marvel film. And so we develop addictions to tales of the miraculous much as we do to heroism.

In defense of miracles, why wouldn't we seek such experiences? Why shouldn't we? Moroni declares that "God has not ceased to be a God of miracles," and that if miracles disappear from our lives, it is only because we "dwindle in unbelief" (Mormon 9:15, 20). In an April 2022 talk in general conference, President Russell M. Nelson went one step further, encouraging Church members to "seek and expect miracles."

I embrace that counsel; I love it. The challenge, for me, comes in applying it. When something miraculous has graced my life, it blows my mind and changes how I see the world and myself. But for that very reason, it exceeds all "seek[ing]" and "expect[ing]." So the thought of expecting miracles—of purporting to understand in advance not only that, but even how they (might) come to be—would cause me to wonder whether I'd witnessed a miracle at all. Might it have been some sleight of mind? Might I have projected it into existence? I think here of the story of a favorite twentieth-century poet, R. S. Thomas, a deep seeker more than a finder of God, who wrote about how his father had gone to a mass faith healing seeking remedy for a physical disability. He experienced a miracle at the meeting and was completely healed. At least until a couple of weeks later, when the disability returned. He later doubted he'd truly been healed at all. That's not the kind of experience for which President Nelson is advocating. And it's not the experience of those who have witnessed true miracles. But it can be the experience of those who "need" them (or who need them "needily").

Struck by this tension between expecting miracles and the surprise that accompanies them, I decided to make miracles an object of my study of the Book of Mormon. What I discovered opened my mind. Yes, we find many miracles there as we conventionally imagine them, with the Book of Mormon itself helping inscribe these conventions in Latter-day Saint thought: heavenly visions (in the book's first chapter), angelic visitations (as early as its third chapter), confounding coincidences (Nephi's confrontation with Laban in the book's fourth chapter), deliverances from danger, life-changing revelations, mass conversions, instantaneous healings, superhuman power, divine guidance, and so much more. Miracles are present even when they might elude our view, undergirding the most pedestrian understanding of the plan of salvation: because God saw that his children "should know concerning the things . . . he had appointed unto" them, "he sent angels to converse with them," taught them "to call on his name," and "made known unto them the plan of redemption" (Alma 12:28–30).

But there are also other species of miracle I had missed in previous readings. Some are slow to cohere, perceptible only over decades or generations, as when Mormon tells us that the Lamanites who were converted "through the preaching of Ammon and his brethren . . . never did fall away" (Alma 23:6). Other miracles are so wide as to escape conscious experience, as when the Lord subtly, almost imperceptibly, "did pour out his Spirit on all the face of the land . . . to prepare [people's] hearts to receive the word" (Alma 16:16). Then there are the incremental accumulations of grace that reveal the chrysalis effects of Christian discipleship, as when Mormon asserts the happiness of "those who died in the faith of Christ" in their old age (Alma 46:41). Irreducible to the "wow" effect of instantaneous recognition, these most impactful miracles were probably never experienced as miracles at all.

This brings me to an important point, still in keeping with President Nelson's admonition to seek miracles while also recalling my father's distinction between heroism and patriotism. Has our passion for spectacle caused us to undervalue miracles we cannot immediately discern, like the act of God that is the simple blessing? I'm not talking the grand ones (e.g., the promise of eternal life or a windfall of unanticipated prosperity), but humbler fare, miracles in miniature. While miracles take myriad forms, blessings are exponentially more diverse and abundant.

Take two small examples. Many would label a medically confounding or rapid recovery from serious illness a miracle. But what about the baseline of good health that gives us everyday life and makes illness seem like such a blight in the first place? That's a blessing—or, better said, a practically uncountable succession of them, day after month after year. Or again, we sometimes hear stories about miraculous opportunities (for jobs or relationships) that come to people after they had nearly lost hope. But what about all the conditions enabling the slow development of capacities, the specialized skills and interpersonal qualities (e.g., for friendship), that convert a momentary windfall into a new reality, making the opportunity possible

and rendering it sustainable? Those would be blessings, a whole diverse array of them.

Look, I can be as turned off as the next person by trite counsel to count our blessings. But their sheer plenitude is startling, and I find their affective difference from miracles (at least of the spectacular variety) provocative. Consider the effects of genuine miracles: Jesus raised Lazarus and doubters believed; David Whitmer beheld the golden plates and thus defended the Book of Mormon even after falling out with Joseph Smith. Miracles shock us into awareness and therefore almost compel our agency. By witnessing God's hand, we feel ourselves snapped into obedience.

Blessings also reveal an attentive God, though they bear a lighter touch. They enter consciousness not as exclamation points but as question marks: Did I notice? How did the blessing arrive? What does it say about its Giver? They thus awaken different impulses of response. For instance, I come home, see my daughter, think, "She's so amazing, what a blessing" . . . and feel prompted to ask her whether I can take her to dinner. Or I find myself graced with a new idea

*Colby Sanford*

for a writing project, consider other deadlines . . . and find a way to carve out a little extra time for the new essay. Or I feel moved by someone's vulnerability in a talk at church, feel blessed by their insights . . . and am moved to text the speaker to express my gratitude. Other blessings, even subtler, pass more fleetingly across consciousness: sharp afternoon sunlight that diversifies the green of dancing leaves; the sweetness of a ripe mango; the casual smile of a longtime friend. Such graces make little outward demand on us, but they gently call something forth in us. In connecting us more deeply to our surroundings, they reveal or at least suggest a world designed for our partnership with God and others.

In this way, blessings elicit facets of our divine nature. One might even say that blessings resonate in a special way with Latter-day Saint theology. I think of it like this: If miracles carry an aura of necessity, then blessings evoke God's pleasure. They are the grace of small accents on God's works of art and on his children. Miracles reveal a God at work, a God willing us to do something specific, whereas blessings feel more like God at play, creating lovely things simply because God is a creative and loving being—as we are and might more fully become. Hence, while miracles evoke a God profoundly different from us, blessings reveal a God with whom we share a common nature, one we might more fully cultivate. To that extent, blessings always come to us from our future.

I'm grateful for miracles. I hope to have many more stories of them to share as the years pass. But I'm increasingly grateful for the smallest ones, blessings—for the ways they awaken me spiritually by drawing me gently into fuller attention. For the ways they reveal God not in occasional lightning flashes of operatic brilliance but rather in the chiaroscuro and matted pink of slow dawn. Blessings, small and simple things, deepen my love for a God whose boundless creativity can be so quiet, so delicate—so exquisitely beautiful. ✳

HL. MARIA MAGDALENA

*Maria Magdalena*

NIKOLA SARIĆ

# WHEN THERE IS NO CROSS TO SEE

*Godly Encounters on the Camino de Santiago*

**FLEUR VAN WOERKOM**

WHEN I STEPPED INTO A DARK chapel in Navarrete, Spain, I didn't expect to see so much gold. The altarpiece was an expansive display of intricate metalwork framing images of Christ, and the glinting gold reflected a distinct brightness. I removed my backpack and sat on a bench, looking up to the crucifixes and cherubs which adorned the ceiling, as other pilgrims came and went. Each time the wooden doors of the chapel eased open, I heard quiet exclamations followed by silent awe. None of us had expected this small earthen town rising above endless grapevines to hold such artistry, reverence, and adoration.

For centuries, various routes of El Camino de Santiago have led pilgrims towards the Catedral Basilica de Santiago de Compostela, the traditional burial place of St. James the Great, located in the northwest corner of Spain. Today, people of many faiths follow paths marked by shells and yellow arrows which wind through hills of grapes and sunflowers, flat desert stretches, modern cities, near-empty villages, and mountainous greenery. The symbol of the cross forms an integral element of the landscape and remains a constant even as the scenery changes. Pilgrims are met by simple sticks stuck through wire fences

in the shape of the cross, stone-carved crucifixes welcoming pilgrims to new regions, and wooden crosses raised high against every horizon. These markers make it impossible to travel even one mile without remembering Jesus Christ.

Growing up, many of my elementary school field trips were visits to Spanish missions along El Camino Real, a trail of Catholic faith along the coast of California. These places always held a sort of dark mysticism for me, and my memory is full of images of candlelit pews and childish games of breath-holding as we tiptoed past the chapel graveyards.

During Sunday School lessons on the Atonement of Jesus Christ, I recall hearing teachers explain that the Church of Jesus Christ of Latter-day Saints doesn't use the symbol of the cross in a way that made the cross seem almost forbidden, an image that should be avoided. It seemed to me that, in an effort to differentiate the restored gospel from other historical Christian traditions, any differences were used to point out flaws in the faith of others, rather than to praise people's innate desire for the sacred.

One day as I walked the red dirt road leading into Astorga, a city near the end of an interminable desert stretch of the Camino, a fellow pilgrim

**The man told me, "I came here wanting to connect with God, but I've been connecting more with people." I replied, "Those sound sort of the same."**

asked me, "So, what do you think about God?" In the conversations I'd held with other pilgrims, hardly anyone had so readily brought up the topic. This man explained that his decision to walk the Camino had been extremely last-minute—mere days after asking a priest at his local church if he thought doing so would be a good idea, he'd started walking towards the alleged grave of St. James.

In an effort to answer his question about God, I described an experience I'd had in Burgos, a city I had passed through earlier on my journey. The cathedral there was of a gorgeous Gothic design, blindingly bright in the sun, and heavily embellished both inside and out. In direct contrast to

*Sarah Hawkes*

the overall beauty, within a small chamber off the cathedral's cloister, I'd found a sculptural depiction of Christ that made me reexamine the symbol of the cross. Unlike the many uplifting depictions of the resurrected Christ that had graced the walls of my church growing up, and contrasting even with the more somber paintings of His sufferings in Gethsemane and His death on the cross, this crucifix was gory. There were splatters of blood and a darkness under the skin that clearly communicated tangible suffering. The physical realness of the cross and Christ's corporeal pain were made achingly clear, making me feel a sadness and despair in the face of death that the paintings in my childhood church had never approached.

Every day along the Camino I observed the physicality required to move and the quickness with which health and vitality can disappear in the aging bodies of pilgrims older than I. So far in my own life, I had experienced levels of physical pain and discomfort—strained muscles, a broken bone, grievous sunburn, sickness, exhaustion—but no matter the severity of those sensations, nothing had come remotely close to the pain that accompanies actual death. It was a concept inconceivable for me to conceptualize. Meditating on the impossibility of life after death, of peace after suffering, of movement after definite stillness, I felt a greater need to believe in the miracle of Christ's Atonement. The crosses dotting my horizon each day became reminders that belief in the incomprehensible bad is what makes room for belief in the unimaginable good.

As we continued walking together, the man told me, "I came here wanting to connect with God, but I've been connecting more with people." I replied, "Those sound sort of the same."

In my conversations with other pilgrims, I found that most people were walking the Camino because they wanted a change in their life or weren't sure what they wanted to do next. A man from Italy told me that he was walking because he and his friends had pledged either to have a child or walk the Camino by the time they reached the age of thirty, and he'd chosen the Camino. A woman from Slovenia wanted to live with greater purpose and hoped to find that purpose on a winding trail through Spain. Another woman carried not only her own prayers but the prayers of friends and family; she walked on behalf of all who knew she was making the pilgrimage, hoping that her arrival in Santiago would bring desired answers and miracles. While my brief encounters with other pilgrims didn't make me privy to all the painful details of their lives, we always voiced our hopes. Each person that I met became a symbol of confidence, sureness, and trust as we cheered each other on.

My personal reasons for walking the Camino included a desire for physical challenge, as well as uncertainty about my future plans. Spending the majority of my time outside and passing constant reminders of Jesus Christ in the shapes of crosses and cathedrals quickly pointed my thoughts toward the spiritual, but that hadn't been my initial purpose. I soon realized that I had left my home in Utah, a desert full of churches, in search of unfamiliarity—only to find myself in another desert full of churches, albeit of a different tradition.

I laughed at myself when I realized this irony, sitting in the dark chapel in Navarrete, looking up at gold and crosses and figures of Christ. Both the Latter-day Saint and Catholic traditions hold harm in their histories; I knew that no organization that claims to follow the teachings of Jesus Christ does so perfectly. The missions I'd visited in California were proof of bad being done in the name of God, as the Spanish forced the Indigenous peoples to adopt the practice of Christianity; the circumstances complicating my current feelings about religion are proof of hurt still being inflicted today. But on the Camino, as an outsider observing the landscape of another religion, and removed from my own faith's largest gathering places, this harm and hurt fell away—not into oblivion, not gone without reckoning, but crowded out by the enormousness of Christ and the goodness of individuals.

It was raining on the morning I set out from Sarria, a city located about one hundred kilometers from the Camino's end. Also starting from Sarria that morning was a group of Spaniards dressed in brightly embroidered clothing. They were fresh and energetic, clearly embarking on the first day of their journey. I passed them as

they gathered to pray outside the walls of a cemetery, and after walking down a steep hill, I paused to watch them descend together—a pipe player leading them at the front, their exuberant brightness breaking out in gallops and shouts of song.

I clapped along with the piper's music as they neared, and one of them pointed at me with a smile. "You dance!" he commanded, so I did. People crossing a bridge pressed to one side to let us pass, skipping and mud-splashing to the notes of the pipe. The dancing man said to me, "When there is darkness in your mind, you continue dancing. When there is blood on your feet, you continue dancing." His instructions continued as we danced down the trail, each time ending with the same words: you continue dancing. He finally slowed and looked in my eyes to ensure my

## "When there is darkness in your mind, you continue dancing. When there is blood on your feet, you continue dancing."

complete attention. "No matter what happens, when we hear the music, we continue dancing. That is *el propósito*. The purpose. You understand?"

As I walked on, the piper's music growing soft behind me, my fingers twirled in the air when I couldn't dance with my feet. I saw the group a few more times throughout that day, and they were always full of song, full of dance, full of encouragement for the strangers they passed. It was clear that their purpose was to have so much joy in their journey that anyone they met would have no choice but to smile. They were a source of unimaginable good for so many pilgrims who were beginning to suffer after weeks of physical and mental exertion.

Clouds parted as I reached Santiago de Compostela after days of cold rain. I walked into the cathedral's plaza alone and sat in the center, resting on my backpack, watching other pilgrims stream in from all sides. They came through the tunnel with the constant song of bagpipes, out

## Like the cross of Christ, which caused His death and necessitated His resurrection, all other finalities must be passed through and remembered.

of streets filled with souvenir shells and sugar-dusted cakes, and I realized that I recognized a surprising number of them. I waved to some and watched others wave to the people they saw and recognized—a widely woven net of knowing. One man in a blue jacket caught everyone's attention: he leaned heavily on his walking sticks, so dependent on them bearing his weight that he eventually fell to his knees. His hands moved between his tearing eyes and too-big heart. No one knew what he cried for, how long he had walked, the prayers he'd carried, or the solace he might have been seeking. We only knew that he knelt in worship of the God who had miraculously brought him there, and in watching, we worshiped with him.

The next morning at pilgrim mass, I watched the priests swing the *botafumeiro* through the transept, incense rising like sacred whispers to heaven. The smoky air, Latin song, and rain-darkened windows distilled that same medieval mysticism that I have always associated with Catholicism. As I stood to accept the small sacramental wafer, I thought of the unthinkable faith it must take to believe in the literal doctrine of transubstantiation—but then, there is unthinkable faith required to believe in anything. I looked around at the other pilgrims, a majority of whom also appeared to be guests in this faith ritual that we had all chosen to take part in, wondering what miracles they'd been hoping for and how many of us had been those miracles for one another. A woman next to me pointed at the priests and whispered, "It used to make me so mad knowing only men could do that, and it still does, but now I try to feel compassion for them, like Christ would. They are only trying their best in a system that isn't perfectly fair."

I spent the rest of that day watching pilgrims arrive in the plaza and wandering past shops selling shells and crosses: reminders that I had come to the end. But the end, once I left it, would become a meridian. Like the cross of Christ, which caused His death and necessitated His resurrection, all other finalities must be passed through and remembered. In the plaza, looking up at the spires of crossed metal, I mourned the loss I'd soon feel when that symbol would cease to occupy so much of my daily view, when there would be no cross to look at.

*Sarah Hawkes*

As rain clouds darkened, my eyes fell from heaven to the slick ground beneath me, and I followed others to the safe dryness of the bagpipe tunnel. We pressed close, strangers making room for each other, laughing and unalone. Each body surrounding mine loomed large and real and alive. Their hearts pumped blood I could not see, held joys and fears I could not name. We all surely held beliefs and prejudices that, if shared, would clash in contradiction, but for many of us, our linguistic limitations prevented such complications. Up close, breath to heaving breath, we all just needed air. This desperate demand distilled the gift of the cross into each person's being and illuminated the simplicity that grew in its wake. Christ's aliveness would be our livelihood, His miraculous contradictions the anchorage of our covenants to take care of each other without judgment or retribution. This was the dance we would continue dancing while looking up to heaven and out at each other; full of darkness and blood, yes, but heartened and looking for every wave of light. ✳

# THE IMAGE OF HEAVEN

*Communion as a Visionary Work of Art*

ROBERT SONNTAG

## THE NEPHITE COSMIC CIRCLE

GATHERED IN THE COURTS OF the temple, the crowd of thousands was now too tired to understand Jesus's words. For hours since he appeared they had waited and watched as each person embraced him to feel his wounded side, clasped his hands to feel the tokens there, and knelt before him to touch his feet. Only after that intimate ceremony did Jesus teach them his law in a long discourse. Having exhausted their ability to listen and comprehend, he prepared to leave, but then delayed when he saw their longing for him to stay. He lingered and taught them in ways deeper than speech. He healed the sick, and then carefully organized the congregation into formation. He brought the children near to him, then moved himself to stand in the midst of them. After kneeling in prayer with the crowd encircling him, and after blessing each child, Jesus directed the adults to look toward the inner circle and behold their little ones. As they did so, the concentric structure into which they had been arranged by Jesus was complemented by heaven, as angels encircled the children and fire encircled the angels.

What was the purpose of this? Why such care in the arrangement? Some things jump out as meaningful: Jesus's deliberate placement of the people, and the specificity of the location of the angels and fire, and the explicit concentricity and circularity of the attendees. What was Jesus trying to teach?

The description reminds me at once of the kinds of ancient universal maps which placed the most sacred site at the center and laid creation out from that axis. A congregation arranged in tiers of holiness with their God at the center could be seen as a kind of living temple. As a temple, It is also an image of Eden: God at the center as the fruit of the tree of life, surrounded in turn by circular concourses of innocent children, of angels and fire echoing the cherubim holding flaming swords, and finally by the adult congregation symbolically outside of Eden. This was also an image of what Jesus called "my doctrine" in his earlier sermon, for those who would draw near to Christ must be baptized by fire, receive the tongue of angels, and become as little children.[1] It was a ritualized vision, using the people to both

*An interpretation of the Nephite gathering, by the author, colorized by Summer C. Christensen & Londan Duffin.*

# I worried that if my physical senses were unreliable, then my spiritual perceptions might likewise be vulnerable to dysfunction and impairment.

create the intended image and be the receivers, commanded to *behold* it. Things which had been explained in words—ideas and metaphors previously not visible to their natural eyes—were now made visible, palpable, spatial, and alive.

## THE NEPHITE EUCHARIST

In that same tiered cosmic circle, perhaps after the angels had withdrawn, the congregation sat and ate bread and wine. A chapter break which did not exist in the original text obscures the continuity between the shape of the gathering and the Lord's supper. When we ignore that artificial break in the text, the circular gathering appears to be Jesus's preparation for the meal to follow.

This type of springtime feast was a common rite all over the ancient world. At the end of the year after Jesus's death observant Israelites would be observing Passover, a pilgrimage feast in which people gathered at the mother temple. Those gathering might have in mind earlier spring feasts at which God joined the feast, such as when Abraham and Sarah had served fresh cakes to their heavenly visitors in the presence of Jehovah and received his promise that they would conceive,[2] or when Moses and seventy elders ate and drank in Mount Sinai in the presence of Jehovah.[3] These and thousands of other similar sacramental meals were among the central purposes of ancient temples the world over. As people prayed and ate together, the feasts were visions of heavenly atonement, an echo of the unity among the divine council in eternity, and a foretaste of the day when heaven and earth will meet again in a feast of reunion. They reached both backward and forward in time, collapsing history, futurity, and the present into the eternal

moment, gathering the bodies of worshippers into an image and extension of the divine council on earth in the presence of God.[4] The Greeks called their temple feasts the *panegyria*, the gathering of all in a circle. As the Nephites encircled their divine king at the temple a year after his sacrificial death at the last Passover, they kept the ancient custom of the feast.

We saints claim to do weekly the sacrament the Nephites were taught to do by Jesus at Bountiful, occasionally referencing 3 Nephi 18 as an articulation of the meaning of our ritual; but we certainly don't take such care in our arrangement, nor include chapter 17's events in our explanations. Our informal weekly meetings are the product of centuries of Protestant iconoclasm in the religious upbringing of most early Latter-day Saints. By "informal" I don't mean that our gatherings are not ritualized nor our interactions often rote. I mean we do not purposefully shape our weekly gatherings into a physical form that reveals their underlying purpose. We are so informal that we are prone to overlook such visions even when described dramatically, as in 3 Nephi 17 and 18. By contrast our temple worship is formal, an acting-out of visions of individual ascent: we progress up the hierarchy of being and physically upward in space,[5] endowed with ritual clothing, surrounded by symbolic images, gathered briefly in our own cosmic circles of prayer and communion. What would our sacrament look like if it were administered as Christ did for the Nephites, with visionary form, as temple worship? If we had a vivid example, perhaps we could better see the divine pattern hidden beneath our own informality.

In fact, we have an excellent model of the celebration of this archetypal feast, with thousands of years of helpful documentation to help us explore it: the weekly liturgy of traditional Christians.

## THE LORD'S SUPPER AS A TEMPLE RITUAL

The Christian celebration of the Lord's supper, called the "Divine Liturgy" in the eastern tradition and "Mass" in the west, is temple worship strikingly similar to that of the Nephites at Bountiful:

*The iconostasis of Saints Peter and Paul Orthodox Church in Salt Lake City, with the divine council represented in the Holy of Holies beyond.*

held in spaces modeled on the Tabernacle of Moses, with public instruction from the Gospels followed by the stratification of the congregation in symbolic tiers of holiness and privacy, overseen by robed officiants acting as icons of Christ and his holy angels, with the intent of bringing about real and intimate communion between heaven and earth.

Early Jewish Christians treated the ritual of the Lord's Supper as a continuation of the priestly ministration of the Jerusalem Temple.[6] Their public preaching and teaching happened on the Jewish sabbath at the synagogue, while they met privately in homes on the following day, the Lord's day, for the holy feast. When later Christians began building dedicated spaces for worship, they modeled their chapels and churches on the tabernacle of Moses, with narthexes, naves, and sanctuaries corresponding to the tabernacle's courtyard, Holy Place, and Holy of Holies, respectively.[7]

As in the earlier tabernacle, access to sanctified spaces in Christian temples was mediated by ritual. The tabernacle had been patterned after the mountaintop vision of Moses, the throne of God in the center of all things and material creation flowing outward from there in a descending cascade of holiness.[8] As YHWH had been envisioned enthroned in the Holy of Holies of heaven's temple surrounded by the divine council, in early churches the priests surrounded the Bishop seated on the *synthronon*, a tiered semicircular structure behind the altar in the most holy place in the church.[9] During the public portion of the liturgy representing Christ's incarnation and mortal teaching, the whole congregation sat in the nave together as the officiant read scripture—emphasizing Christ's teaching as recorded in the New Testament Gospels—and gave a homily or discourse. After the public liturgy the deacons would forcibly dismiss the unbaptized:

> *"Those who are catechumens [not yet baptized], depart; catechumens depart; all those who are catechumens, depart. Let none of the catechumens remain."*

As the catechumens withdrew and the bishop consecrated the bread and wine, the gathering gave body to the same cosmic pattern by which Christ arranged the Nephites: the unbaptized at the perimeter, those "little ones"[11] who had been baptized by fire in the Holy Place being ministered to by angels, and Christ at the center of focus in the Holy of Holies. As the High Priest had carried the holy blood of YHWH out of the Holy of Holies on the Day of Atonement to sanctify and renew creation, the Bishop and the angelic attendants carried the consecrated gifts through the chancel screen in a vision of Christ's second coming.

It is that theophanic aim which most clearly marks traditional Christian liturgy as temple worship: to bring about atonement between Christ and his people, including their personal communion with him and their dawning godhood as his reborn children. After unveiling the body and blood of Christ on the altar, the priest in the Nestorian liturgy says *"my eyes have seen the King, the Lord of hosts. How terrible is this place, for today*

*I have seen the Lord face to face, and this is nothing if not the house of God, and this is the gate of heaven."*[12] For Orthodox, Catholic, and other traditional Christians, these consecrated gifts become the "real presence" of Christ in the congregation, and at the altar table they are "made worthy of the visitation of God and are united with him."[13] As Christ was a manifestation of both divine masculinity and divine femininity, both "the power of God and the wisdom of God," and as the sacred bread in ancient Israel was always associated with mother Wisdom, the bread is also an invocation of the divine mother.[14] Orthodox Christians recognize this ritual as symbolic of and a catalyst for the transformations of the disciple which bring us through three primary stages of spiritual development: out of a state of willful sin through repentance, through the spirit-enlightened contemplation where we learn to see creation as it really is, and finally into "theological mystagogy": a union with God wherein we are initiated fully into the mysteries. "Those who arrive at this

*The sacrament table and tiered pulpit of the temple in Kirtland. In Kirtland, as in the earliest Christian churches, the seat for the presiding high priest stood at the top and center of the tiered throne.*

*The veil, altar, and synthronon of the church of Panagia Ekatontapiliani in Paros, Greece (5th century). Note that the synthronon is furnished with icons of the divine council.*

stage are raised beyond the limits of created nature; and they attain a union with God that is beyond all sensory, cognitive, and rational apprehension because they are now completely filled by the uncreated and deifying energy of God, and become God by grace.["15]

If I were explaining Latter-day Saint temple worship to an Orthodox Christian, I would say that our ceremonies are comparable to the consecration and enthronement of a bishop that prepares him to officiate in the ordinances of the Divine Liturgy. The ritual culminates in the individual's or couple's ritual theophanic union with God and ritual qualification to administer in ordinances which reach beyond the veil. A similarly brief explanation of the Divine Liturgy for Latter-day Saints would be that it is the communal counterpart to our largely individual temple worship: The ancient temple was the setting for both individual priestly initiation rites (washing, anointing, clothing, consecration), and for communal worship and atonement. The initiation and endowment of individual priests was not the ultimate aim of ancient temple liturgy; the true objective was the sanctifying communal worship that those priests would be qualified to facilitate. Continuing that same tradition, the Christian Divine Liturgy aims not only to bring individuals up to God and prepare them for divine service, but ultimately to bind all creation together in one

in Christ. Today's Latter-day Saints ritually seal some isolated relationships in that communion, sealing spouse to spouse and parent to child, but we never formally enact the feast of communion which actually brings the whole cosmos together.

More precisely I should say that we *no longer* formally enact it, because this formalized feast was the primary function of temples built by Joseph Smith. Unlike later temples built with successive chambers for small groups of individual initiates to be endowed, Joseph Smith's temples were built with open plans for communal worship. Like ancient churches, they were laid out cosmically with a separable Holy of Holies. As in the first Christian temples, that Holy of Holies featured a sacramental altar and possibly the first true *synthronon* built since the Byzantine era.[15]

While the building could adapt by the drawing of fabric veils to individual initiation and small group instruction, it is the communion feast which was built into the wood and stone of the building. Though we still administer the sacrament, it has been carefully de-formalized: sacrament tables are moved to the side of the chapel with an empty pulpit at the front and center, iconography has been vigilantly eliminated, communion is held before teaching rather than as the culmination of it, and there is no formal verbalization of the eschatological or transcendent unions symbolized by the rite.

## ENVISIONING COSMIC MORMONISM

We find more windows into this vision as we examine the early years of the Latter-day Saint movement. In Joseph Smith's teaching, "sealing" did much more than solemnize unions within nuclear families or to our dead ancestors along genealogical lines. He spoke more frequently of being sealed to the fathers and mothers who are in heaven,[17] and taught that Christ would visit the faithful and "seal you his."[18] He predicted a future gathering between the earthly saints, their redeemed dead, and all members of the divine council at the end of the world, when the family of God takes possession of the Earth as in the beginning.[19] This is the gathering of all things in one in Christ: the living and dead, earthly and heavenly, creation and creator. When priests and priestesses are endowed in Latter-day Saint temples, it is ultimately in symbolic preparation to walk themselves and others through the ordinances of this cosmic atonement:

> D&C 107:18 *The power and authority of the higher, or Melchizedek Priesthood, is to hold the keys of all the spiritual blessings of the church—*
>
> 19 *To have the privilege of receiving the mysteries of the kingdom of heaven, to have the heavens opened unto them, to commune with the general assembly and church of the Firstborn, and to enjoy the communion and presence of God the Father, and Jesus the mediator of the new covenant.*

Whether we actually grow into that invitation to become officiators is dependent, we are told in the ritual, on our own faithfulness.

That eschatological feast is the same divine moment sought by Christians in their weekly liturgy. In Orthodox Christianity, before it is baked the communion loaf is stamped—the Orthodox say "sealed"—with the image of Christ, of Mary the mother in heaven, of the nine angelic orders. When it is sacrificed, those portions are divided up and placed deliberately on the communion plate. Additional bread is then torn and arranged for the living and the dead and placed before the pieces representing the heavenly members of the divine council. Each group is mentioned carefully in prayer as the bread is dismembered.

A small cosmic architectural dome (the *asteriscos* or "star cover") is then placed over the plate, completing the revelation of the bread as a vision of the cosmic communion in the temple. It is a small icon of the congregation in the church, worshiping before the icons of Christ, Mary, and the saints and angels of heaven. The bread is further dis-membered as it is distributed and then re-membered as the congregation comes together in unity and love in Christ. Orthodox Christians see the icon of All Saints as an image of the communion sought during the liturgy: [20]

Shining through the Nephites' circle at Bountiful and the Divine Liturgy of traditional Christians, this is the vision underlying our own Sunday sacrament, waiting for eyes to see it.

## BECOME A SEER

At both the Nephite and traditional Christian communions we are invited to see

A general assembly . . . [21]

At which the gospel message is ritually read to prepare for communiony . . .

Arranged in the same cosmic structure as the Garden of Eden and Moses's Tabernacley . . .

With the initiated brought higher upward and inward within the ontological structurey . . .

With angels present to minister and witnessy . . .

With the initiated eating and drinking in the presence of Christy . . .

*Above: The image of the seal laid on the bread: Christ in the center, with Mary to his right hand, and with nine triangles for the nine angelic choirs. Below: the dismembered portions of bread laid out on the communion plate. Colorized by Summer C. Christensen.*

Enjoying a foretaste of the glorious final atonement between those in heaven and those on earth, the gods and their childreny . . .

Expressed in a work of living art using the bodies of the participants.

It is unlikely that the format of Latter-day Saint sacrament meetings will change to better disclose this sublime vision. More likely, you must learn to see it for yourself and to allow it to transform your approach to Wisdom's table. Once seen, this vision will change not only how you worship on Sunday, but how creation shines forth to you moment to moment. Like Nephi after his ascent or Enoch after washing his eyes, you will learn to perceive the patterns of being not visible to the natural eye.[22] In an echo of Alma the Younger,[23] seventh-century monk and theologian St. Maximus the Confessor taught that the initiation into the mystery of communion symbolized the dawning of seership in the faithful; they were to learn to see beyond the material world into the mysteries—the invisible patterns governing all things—culminating in the vision of and union with God.[24]

Someday you may be invited to a feast that reflects the image of heaven so perfectly that heaven itself shakes with gladness and cannot be withheld from attending.[25] May we have our eyes opened by God to see that invitation when it arrives. In the meantime, I pray that each day finds us more prepared to officiate, prepared to gather and conduct all creation around us in the right praise of God. ✳

1.  3 Nephi 11:33–38.

2.  Genesis 18:1–15.

3.  Exodus 24:1–11.

4.  The archetype of the new year temple festival, the "year rite," has been thoroughly described with vivid examples by many scholars. See Mircea Eliade, "Sacred Time and Myths," in *The Sacred and the Profane: The Nature of Religion*, trans. Willard R. Trask (New York: Harcourt, 1959), 68–115; Hugh Nibley, "The Hierocentric State," in *The Collected Works of Hugh Nibley*, vol. 10, *The Ancient State* (Salt Lake City: Deseret Book, 1991); John Lundquist, "What is a Temple? A Preliminary Typology," and Brian Hauglid, "Sacred Time and the Temple," in *Temples of the Ancient World*, ed. Donald W. Parry (Salt Lake City: Deseret Book, 1994), 83–117, 636–43.

5.  Contemporary Latter-day Saint temple designs deemphasize or eliminate this upward movement, but it was a prominent feature of many earlier temples.

6.  Margaret Barker, "The Temple Roots of the Liturgy," MargaretBarker.com, 2000.

7.  The earliest Christian church building yet discovered, built around 300 AD in Aqaba, Jordan, reflects this arrangement.

8.  Margaret Barker, "Beyond the Veil of the Temple. The High Priestly Origin of the Apocalypses," MargaretBarker.com, 1998.

9.  At the moment of enthronement the congregation sang the "trisagion hymn," including the acclamation of "holy, holy, holy" to God on his throne, just as the cherubim in Isaiah 6 did in their worship in the heavenly temple. The earthly congregation echoes the adoration of the heavenly, creating a vision of the divine council.

10. "The Divine Liturgy of Saint John Chrystostom," Liturgical Texts of the Orthodox Church, Greek Orthodox Archdiocese of America. Catechumens in most Orthodox liturgies are now welcome to stay and observe most Eucharist services, though the formal dismissal may still be announced to preserve the cosmic structure of the gathering.

11. Matthew 18:6; "little ones" here includes all those who had become like little children.

12. "Nestorian Liturgy: The Hallowing of Addai and Mari Disciplers of the East (The Anaphora of the Blessed Apostles)," Nestorian.org.

13. Father Maximos Constas, "The Body as Ritual Space," Lecture at the 2022 Colloquium on the Mystagogy of St. Maximos the Confessor, April 28–30, 2022, available on YouTube.

14. 1 Corinthians 1:24; Proverbs 9:1–5; Barker "Temple Roots of the Liturgy."

15. Father Maximos Constas, "Body as Ritual Space."

16. In the Holy of Holies of the heavenly temple, Joseph Smith envisioned a large multiseated throne (JST Revelation 4:4, 6). When the divine council attended the feast at Kirtland, they appeared as traditional Christians would expect: atop the *synthronon* built per Joseph's vision (D&C 110).

17. Refer to his sermons of August 13, 1843, and March 10, 1844, for his identification of the "fathers" of Malachi's prophecy with these heavenly patriarchs. "Discourse, 13 August 13, 1843—A, as reported by William Clayton," and "Discourse, 10 March 1844, as Reported by Wilford Woodruff," Joseph Smith Papers.

18. Mosiah 5:15.

19. JST Genesis 9:21–25; Moses 7:62–65.

20. "All Saints Icon | The Great Cloud of Witnesses," July 1, 2013, A Reader's Guide to Orthodox Icons.

21. Hebrews 12:23, from the Greek *panegyris*, meaning "the gathering of all in a circle."

22. 1 Nephi 11:36; Moses 6:35–36.

23. 1 Nephi 11:36; Moses 6:35–36.

24. Saint Maximus the Confessor, *On the Ecclesiastical Mystagogy,* trans. Jonathan J. Armstrong (Yonkers: St. Vladimir's Seminary Press, 2019), 82–85.

25. JST Genesis 9:22–23.

# DEDICACIÓN

CITLALLI H
XOCHITIOTZIN
ORTEGA

*En Español:*

*Escrito el Domingo 19 de mayo 2024 en la dedicación del Templo de Puebla México.*

Al pisar tu casa
Toda miel borda las luminarias del alma/
al pisar/
eternidad acaricia/
estás con nosotros-brillo de oro-
-dialogas-
el tiempo no existe.
Cubres inmensamente/
    Vuelo y vocablo.

Inclino mi alma/
      en el panal brillante de tus frutos
    -balbuceo mariposa de polen-
Todo lo eres en el delicado susurro.

Eternos astros/
brillan en la inteligencia pura de tu bendición.

Padre/
inclino, inclino mi alma.

*In English:*

*Written on Sunday, May 19, 2024, at the dedication of the Puebla Mexico Temple.*

On entering your house,
the soul's lights are rimmed with honey
On entering,
eternity caresses.
You are with us—in golden brilliance—
—you commune with us—
time does not exist.
Your covering extends over
    flight and phrase.

I bow my soul
    In the bright honeycomb of your fruits,
  a pollen-gathering butterfly babbles
everything you are in a delicate whisper.

Eternal stars
shine in the pure intelligence of your blessing.

Father
I bow, I bow my soul.

# CLOTHING OURSELVES IN CHRIST

DEIDRE
NICOLE
GREEN

**FULL DISCLOSURE: I LOVE WEARING** garments. I know this is not everybody's stance, but it is mine. After receiving my endowment over twenty years ago, I had the experience a lot of people have—I was somewhat stunned and unsure what to make of it. Since we were given less information about what to expect back then, I remember being surprised and puzzled, and although I could feel that something was fundamentally different about me afterwards (I've been

*William Blake*

teased for publicly characterizing this change as an "ontological shift"), I couldn't quite make sense of the temple ceremony and was not eager to repeat the experience (though my evolving love for temple worship belongs in a separate essay entirely). Yet even in the stunned and sober state in which I remained for a few days following, I was thrilled to wear garments. I remember standing over the washing machine in my parents' home and (rather obsessively and perfectionistically) asking my beloved maternal grandmother for guidance on how to wash them correctly because I didn't want to risk any damage to them or disrespect them. I felt an innate reverence for them. In a way I could not begin to explain at twenty-one, I felt at home in the garment; I felt as if I had *come* home, as if I had come home to myself or *become* myself in a new way now that I inhabited this sacred, religious clothing. Through both personal experience and scholarly reflection, I have come to believe that the garment is formative of our subjectivity, that wearing the garment symbolizes our willingness to let Christ shape our very selfhood. In what follows, I explore a theology of the garment that can help us make meaning of its role in our lives of discipleship in the twenty-first century.

Recently, Church leaders have initiated and engaged in more discussion about the garment in general conference and other venues. Latter-day Saints have been reminded that "we find Jesus . . . in the symbolism of the garment."[1] Young Women General President Emily Belle Freeman explains in her October 2023 general conference talk that she wears "the holy garment as a constant reminder" of her covenants and her choice to walk the covenant path with Jesus Christ "because I want to live in committed covenant relationship with Him."[2] President Russell M. Nelson declares, "When you put on your garment, you may feel that you are truly putting upon yourself the very sacred symbol of the Lord Jesus Christ—His life, His ministry, and His mission, which was to atone for every [child] of God."[3] Perhaps even more pointedly, in a recent BYU devotional, Elder Allen D. Haynie teaches that the most important of the multiple symbolic meanings of the garment is "a remembrance of the Savior's sacrifice in the Garden of Gethsemane and on the cross and His glorious Resurrection."[4] J. Anette Dennis, First Counselor in the General Relief Society Presidency, further explains both how garments tie to the Atonement of Jesus Christ and how through them he becomes interwoven with our very identities:

> The garment of the holy priesthood is deeply symbolic and *also* points to the Savior. When Adam and Eve partook of the fruit and had to leave the Garden of Eden, they were given coats of skins as a covering for them. It is likely that an animal was sacrificed to make those coats of skins— symbolic of the Savior's own sacrifice for us. *Kaphar* is the basic Hebrew word for atonement, and one of its meanings is "to cover." Our temple garment reminds us that the Savior and the blessings of His Atonement cover us throughout our lives. As we put on the garment of the holy priesthood each day, that beautiful symbol *becomes a part of us.* [5]

Through wearing the garment, and doing so whenever possible, Jesus Christ and his Atonement exert constant influence on us and shape our subjectivity, becoming a part of who we are.

In my essay entitled "Enveloping Grace," I discuss Christ and his Atonement as enveloping and containing us as individuals. Drawing on the thought of feminist theologian Serene Jones and others, I argue that sin, as well as social and cultural forces, can leave a person diffuse, dissolute, and fragmented rather than held together in a coherent whole as a subject. Jones and other feminists highlight that this dissolution of the self may be a problem particularly for women, who are socialized to give so much of themselves to others and to identify so much with the needs, desires, and objectives of others that they lose themselves. Gender is, of course, not the only

## I felt at home in the garment; I felt as if I had *come* home, as if I had come home to myself or *become* myself in a new way now that I inhabited this sacred, religious clothing.

lens by which to identify the disparate ways in which sin can distort selfhood; process theologian Catherine Keller argues that sin may result in the "soluble self" that I have been describing, which stands in contrast to a "separative self," defined by pride and domination over others.[6] Everyone, regardless of gender, can experience one pattern or the other or oscillate between the two. In any case, Jones theorizes divine grace as that which envelops and thereby contains the multiple and fluid self, thereby preventing them from being "dissolved into the projects, plans, and desires of others," which would leave them "without a 'skin' to define the integrity of [their] personhood." God's grace offers each individual a skin—a divinely gifted envelope—that holds and contains her in a cohesive whole. Insofar as divine grace intends a person's ultimate flourishing, it provides her with a "skin of her own (and God's) best desires" so that she is "clothed in grace."[7]

Jones's theological reflections are influenced by feminist philosopher Luce Irigaray, who articulates women's need for a divinely gifted "envelope" to contain them as a cohesive self so they can find and situate themselves in their own place.[8] According to Irigaray, the first envelope given to a person is the body, which serves as the boundary delineating the individual from other bodies.[9] Irrespective of gender, allowing anyone to be both separate and whole, this corporeal demarcation is especially crucial for women, who tend to become dissolute in response to cultural expectations. This envelope provides self-definition and appropriate boundaries, offering a woman integrity and individual wholeness. Additionally, such a providential envelope protects a woman from adopting inauthentic

> My garment reminds me that as a consecrated being, I have an extra layer of protection from the various social and cultural forces that want to reduce my body—an inextricable part of my soul—to an object of consumption or commodification.

forms of envelopment that she might seek in the world in an effort to construct a false or superficial sense of self-identity, including "clothes, make-up and jewellery."[10] These artificial envelopes prevent her from receiving more authentic forms of envelopment and therefore from establishing more genuine forms of selfhood.

Irigaray's analysis suggests that cultural forces that demean women and erode their corporeal boundaries leave them amorphous and vulnerable so that they need an enhanced mode of envelopment.[11] For Jones, this divinely gifted envelope *is* Christian grace. Adding to the argument made by these feminist thinkers (which centers around women but is just as productively conceived in terms of the soluble self)—that the containment or envelopment that grace provides functions to hold together the soluble self as an individual with integrity, rather than dissolving into a diffuse and amorphous self—I would say that grace also can function to contain the separative self from overreaching bounds and doing harm to others. In this way, the garment symbolizes the way in which Christ can serve as a mediator in all human relationships. He and his grace stand between me and all others, informing and forming those relationships and intersubjectivities. Moreover, in response to the temptation to adopt an artificial envelope in a world that constantly lies to me about the source of my selfhood and value as a person, my garment reminds me that as a consecrated being, I have an extra layer of protection from the various social and cultural forces that

want to reduce my body—an inextricable part of my soul[12]—to an object of consumption or commodification; it endows me with an added power to resist these forces of commodification, serving as a physical buffer and barrier that reminds me that my body belongs to me and its Creator. At the same time, the garment marks me as belonging to a consecrated community, which further highlights the intersubjective nature of becoming a self and a Christian disciple.

The notion of grace as envelopment by the divine resonates with Restoration scripture, which offers multiple depictions of Christ's Atonement and redemption as encircling and enveloping us.[13] For example, Lehi, in testifying that the Lord has redeemed his soul, declares: "I have beheld his glory, and I am encircled about eternally in the arms of his love."[14] For me, there can be no better symbol of the way in which divine grace, made possible through the Atonement of Jesus Christ, contains me as a cohesive self than the garment, which literally offers a second skin to resist the pressure to create a false identity or form a pseudoskin that is merely a product of the fallen world in which I live. The garment restrains the forces that would undo my selfhood. The garment is a tangible reminder that I am constituted as a subject by Christ's grace and *only* by that grace; the grace made possible by the Atonement of Jesus Christ and in relationship to him is the only reason I enjoy selfhood.

That the garment forms my subjectivity helps to explain why wearing it consistently and whenever possible is emphasized by Church leaders. I might think of it as being nearly—or actually—essential to my self. Postcolonial feminist theorist Meyda Yeğenoğlu, writing on the veil worn by Muslim women, observes that religious clothing is "a dress which we might consider as articulating the very identity" of a religious person.[15] According to her, this "sartorial matter" is *not* external to one's identity but rather exists "as a fundamental piece conjoined with the embodied subjectivity" of a person and as part of the body itself,[16] such that she is "*constituted in (and by) the fabric-ation of*" it.[17] For Yeğenoğlu, the impulse to "unveil" the Muslim woman in a liberatory effort can only amount to an imperialist tendency that might threaten the very subjectivity of a religious person whose identity is interwoven with her religious attire. She maintains that conceptualizations of the body, along with bodily presentation and performance, are culturally constructed and therefore culturally specific. Moreover, in keeping with the concern articulated above about artificial forms of envelopment and the commodification of the body by Western capitalism and culture, Yeğenoğlu employs postcolonial critique to reject the application of Western standards to non-Western contexts, opining that Muslim women's religious clothing does not confine or discipline the body to a greater degree than does Western culture: "Emphasizing the culturally specific nature of embodiment reveals . . . that the power exercised upon bodies by veiling is no more cruel or barbaric than the control, supervision, training, and constraining of bodies by other practices, such as bras, stiletto heels, corsets, cosmetics, and so on."[18] This final point helps us to rethink the garment as something that resists the commodification of the body rather than merely something to cover, control, or constrict the body. It suggests that to see the garment as restrictive is to see one cultural standard, namely that of Western capitalism, as natural rather than as a

*William Blake*

cultural construct that does harm to the soul and that to subscribe to that standard is somehow more conducive to freedom than religious dress.

I suggest that the garment is neither a vestige of a magical worldview nor an arbiter of Victorian ideals of modesty; rather, its purpose is to be formative of a person's subjectivity. It forms Latter-day Saints as consecrated individuals and forms us as followers of and in likeness to Christ, who epitomized consecration. The garment is symbolic of the veil of the temple, which is not only symbolic of Christ but is also the place in which we present ourselves before the divine. In an embodied way, we pronounce our total presence, availability, and openness to divine call, the tangible equivalent of verbal exclamations of women and men in the scriptures who played pivotal roles in salvation history by declaring, "Here I am!"[19] Such a pronouncement is to me the essence of consecration, and I believe that the garment represents my perpetual position before the veil, reminding me that I am forever at the disposal of the divine. Moreover, the veil is a place where our utter dependence on God is epitomized: no matter how much I know or think that I know, in this space I always perform epistemic humility, demonstrating my total reliance on God for salvific knowledge, salvation, and exaltation. Ultimately, we come to be subjects only to the degree that we recognize our total dependence on God, and so this reminder is crucial to the process of formation as a subject. The Book of Mormon teaches that the humility that acknowledges this total dependence combined with faith affords "communion with the Holy Spirit,"[20] which is to say that it affords union, mutual relationship, and communication with the Holy Spirit.[21] The garment provides a constant tangible reminder of that dependence and of the intimate relation with deity that is always available to us as we acknowledge that dependence. Wearing the garment demonstrates that we "have clothed [ourselves] with Christ,"[22] put on Christ,[23] and thereby "clothe [ourselves] with the new self, created according to the likeness of God in true righteousness and holiness."[24] In order for the garment to exert its full efficacy in our lives, we must theologize and conceptualize it properly. I believe that as we conceive of the garment as sartorial grace, which we are in constant need of, we can come to be embodied and formed as subjects by Christ and his Atonement. ✳

1. Allen D. Haynie, "Meeting Jesus in the House of the Lord," *Y Magazine,* Spring 2024, 29.

2. Emily Belle Freeman, "Walking in Covenant Relationship with Christ," *Liahona*, November 2023, 79.

3. Russell M. Nelson, "Enter into Thy Closet"; quoted in Haynie, "Meeting Jesus," 29.

4. Haynie, "Meeting Jesus," 28.

5. J. Anette Dennis, "Put Ye On the Lord Jesus Christ," *Liahona*, May 2024, 11, emphasis added.

6. Catherine Keller, *From a Broken Web: Separation, Sexism, and Self* (Boston: Beacon Press, 1986), 13.

7. Serene Jones, *Feminist Theory and Christian Theology: Cartographies of Grace* (Minneapolis: Augsburg Fortress, 2000), 121, 64. See Deidre Nicole Green, "Enveloping Grace," in *Latter-day Saint Perspectives on Atonement*, ed. Deidre Nicole Green and Eric D. Huntsman (Urbana: University of Illinois Press, 2024), 263.

8. Luce Irigaray, "Place, Interval: A Reading of Aristotle, *Physics* IV," in *An Ethics of Sexual Difference,* trans. Carolyn Burke and Gillian C. Gill (Ithaca, NY: Cornell University Press, 1993), 35.

9. Irigaray, "Place, Interval," 36.

10. Luce Irigaray, "Sexual Difference," in *The Irigaray Reader,* ed. Margaret Whitford (Oxford: Blackwell Publishers, 1991), 169–70. See Green, "Enveloping Grace," 261.

11. See Green, "Enveloping Grace," 262.

12. See D&C 88:15.

13. See Green, "Enveloping Grace," 263–64.

14. 2 Nephi 1:15.

15. Meyda Yeğenoğlu, *Colonial Fantasies: Towards a Feminist Reading of Orientalism* (Cambridge: Cambridge University Press, 1998), 119.

16. Yeğenoğlu, *Colonial Fantasies*, 118.

17. Yeğenoğlu, *Colonial Fantasies*, 119, emphasis in the original.

18. Yeğenoğlu, *Colonial Fantasies*, 116.

19. Genesis 22:1; see also Genesis 22:11; 31:11; 46:2; and Luke 1:38.

20. Jarom 1:4.

21. *Oxford English Dictionary*, s.v. "communion (n.)."

22. Galatians 3:27, NRSV.

23. Romans 13:14.

24. Ephesians 4:24, NRSV; see also Colossians 3:10.

# BEYOND DOUBT

*An Interview with Charles Taylor*

*Charles Margrave Taylor, called by some "the most interesting and important philosopher writing in English today," is professor emeritus at McGill University and the author of many notable works on religion, culture, and the self, including* A Secular Age. *Wayfare Editor Zachary Davis invites Taylor to reflect on the development of Taylor's own faith and the impact faith can have on all of us as we act in the world.*

**What are your earliest memories of your spiritual and religious life?**
Well, a lot of the early experience was negative. I was brought up in Quebec, in the French-speaking Catholic Church in Quebec, and at that point it was extremely clerical, extremely authoritarian. So when I was very young I don't remember being impressed one way or another. Although I was impressed by the rhetorical culture that came with the Dominican sermons. It's a kind of rhetoric that I can still conjure up in my mind. It wasn't until I was well into adolescence that I felt called upon to take some kind of stand towards religion, and it seemed to me to be very negative.

A lot of Quebecers had this experience, which eventually came out roughly in the 1960s, what we call the Quiet Revolution, where so many people left the church and there was a de-clericalization. So that could have been my story, but what happened is that a lot of the theological work that underlay what later became Vatican II was being written by French-speaking Jesuits and Dominicans, people like Henri de Lubac and Yves Congar. And because the French and Quebec communities of these orders were so closely linked, some of these texts, some not yet published, some even under ban, got into my hands. And I was really deeply moved and carried away by this completely different picture of the faith in history. It was not focused on worrying about one's own personal salvation, whether you obeyed the rules and so on, but that Christ came to save the world. It was something that was for all of history and for all humanity. I saw a certain vision of a kind of love and self-giving that could really transform not just oneself, but the world. And it had a tremendously powerful effect on me. This was the crucial, decisive turning point in my life.

**If you had a grandchild come to you and say, "Grandpa, I just think Jesus and Christianity is a myth. I'm just going to follow science," how might you respond?**

*Augustus Vincent Tack*

I think I'd say, "Find your own spiritual path, but 'just science' can't be the source of that spiritual path."

**And if that same grandchild says, "Well, Grandpa, spirituality isn't real. Science is real."**

I think I would try to point out that all the things that deeply move us in ethics, in music, in art—science in no way explains that, or even comes to terms with that. That there is another level, another dimension to human experience.

**What relationship should Christians have with doubt?**

My whole life's been accompanied by doubts and uncertainty. I believe faith can be a sister of doubt. You have a sense of the direction you want to move in, and then moments when you don't really move that easily in the direction you want. Faith is a challenge. You can think that it's an intellectual challenge and try to find reasons. But by prayer and by thought—I practice a certain kind of Christian meditation—you can get beyond this, and there's some kind of purification of the faith that happens. That you're reaching out beyond these doubts to a deeper, richer, fuller connection. Faith means that you sense that there's something—and here the vocabulary fails in a certain sense—I was going to say something *out there*, or I could say something is *up there*, or I could say something is *down there* because it's deeper. Or deeper *in there*. The whole field of ethics and the ends of human life are only available through metaphor.

Here's another very powerful experience I had when I was an undergraduate at McGill. There was a remarkable teacher called Wilfred Cantwell

Smith, who did a lot of work in India. He became one of the foremost people in the Christian world who studied Islam. I signed up for his course in comparative religion and it was an absolutely extraordinary experience. He didn't have great rhetorical skill—he kind of walked up and down holding his toga gown while almost mumbling, but he evoked what it was to be a Buddhist or to be a Muslim in an extraordinarily rich way.

And I immediately liked him. There was an ecumenical spirit which only came to fruition and broad acceptance later on in my life. A desire not only to want to understand, but to exchange with other faiths. From Buddhism, for instance, the intuition of *sunyata*—emptiness. That a lot of the things that you're attached to are getting in your way, and if you can kind of fall into an abyss when you detach from them, that is what opens up the gates to something bigger. And so that very Buddhist idea makes sense for me in a Christian perspective. That these kinds of doubts hold you back, and somehow, if you can get beyond them, if you fall into the pit they're threatening, it can allow the greater power of the force and *agape* that I feel is somewhere there in the universe because of the life and death of Christ. So that's the kind of relationship faith can have with doubt, and why I think it's the good sister, not the bad sister, of faith.

**The way you described this world religions course models a way we can hold on to our own faith commitments without being threatened by those that are different.**
Our faith is even enriched by that difference. It's very paradoxical. And to certain people it's totally incomprehensible to think positively of something that is different, or in terms of propositions, contradictory. That to think positively of other faiths must mean you are in the process of moving out of your own faith. But it doesn't have to work that way. It's a great mystery. It's something that I don't claim fully to understand.

**Do you think it has something to do with an intuition that though there are very divergent expressions of the divine or the sacred they point to some common source?**

Yes, yes. *Point to* is maybe too strong, but obviously they must have some kind of common source. And then when you factor in other things, such as the ethical growth in human history, starting off with what Karl Jaspers identified as the Axial Age, these changes in Greece, Israel, the Ganges Plain and China that occurred. They're very different in many ways, but there are certainly very powerful common features. Then you look at the continuing development of ethics over time so that now, for instance, we have an ethic of the United Nations Declaration of Human Rights of 1948, which is way beyond the demands that existed earlier.

And this has obviously been the work of people from all these different traditions. You get the great breakthrough of nonviolence against unjust regimes with Gandhi, a Hindu. And then that is picked up by Martin Luther King and John Lewis, Christians who recognized the resonance of what Gandhi was doing for Christians.

**A compelling reason to me for why we are in fact spiritual (and not merely material) beings is that we do respond to the call to love. And the way that you describe this ethic of love moving across cultures and traditions, being particularized, but nonetheless finding resonance and response in each seems important for understanding the spark of the divinity which is within us.**
Yes, absolutely! We often translate the Greek word *agape* as something to do with the love of parents for children or caring love. It's not quite the same as erotic love nor even the love for parents. I think of this love in terms of Paul's kenotic love, a self-emptying love, a reaching down love. That is the force and that has the power to move people very deeply. So you are right, if you think of pictures of the human psyche which stress the search for power, wealth, and control, etc.— which undoubtedly also exist!—but if you think that is the whole story, the Marxist, materialistic accounts just seem to leave out terribly important facts about human beings.

**We're in an age of anxiety, a pessimistic age, a challenging spiritual age. But at the end**

# Whether you like it or not, you are the time. So when something really holds you or pulls you, you may not understand why, but if there's some genuine contact, God is speaking to our time in you.

**of your book *A Secular Age*, you encourage readers to be unafraid of the future, to trust that the Christian witness can be renewed for each generation. How can we live forward in faith and not be overcome by worry or nostalgia?**

You have to look back on history and take off the blinkers. Some traditionalists in the Catholic Church, for example, believe that the church starts at Pentecost in Israel in the 30s AD and it's continually saying the same thing. Which is obviously absurd when you really know the history. That's what Vatican II really recognized. What we're called upon to do is to continue this history in a way that connects with and makes sense of what we have become. Great saints, such as Saint Paul writing in the New Testament or Teresa of Ávila or Saint John of the Cross or Meister Eckhart still speak to us, so there is a certain kind of continuity, but each age is tremendously different, and the spiritual realities are very different.

**So instead of seeking to recover the original Christian experience or message, we should think of our own lives as part of an unfolding message?**

That's right.

**What does it look like as a Christian to be responsive to our own time?**

Whether you like it or not, you are the time. So when something really holds you or pulls you, you may not understand why, but if there's some genuine contact, God is speaking to our time in you. The original experience is not figuring out, but being pulled. Only later may you develop reasons you can explain to someone else. ✳

# THE BEAUTY OF COMMUNION

## Love as Creative Force

### TERRYL GIVENS

WE TEND TO THINK OF BEAUTY as adornment, as pleasant but inessential. We enjoy a lovely snowscape or a hummingbird's iridescence. Such beauty seemingly provides enjoyable respite during life's brief intermissions, sandwiched between the more meaningful acts of labor, service, and other necessities. Have we by such thinking trivialized the beautiful?

The good and the true seem essential, by comparison. They have solidity and unimpeachable status, purpose. We guide our lives by them, self-evident reference points that they are. We are to choose the good, search out the truth. One might ask, what happens when all truth has been found and embraced, the good clearly seen and realized? What then? How much richness is constituted by a life that only chose between forking paths, a will that constrained itself to no more creativity than a logic gate? Do we achieve the ends of our eternal nature by a repeated process of selection?

The God of Genesis bursts upon the stage of human consciousness through creative activity. We are introduced to the divine nature as that which enlarges the universe by the generation of something new. Even if working with pre-existent matter, new configurations, new arrangements bring forth that which did not exist and now does.

Is what we call the beautiful in reality an assent to the creative impulse of the divine? In his meditation on the magnificence of the created order, the harmony and fittedness and inexhaustible energy of nature in all its variety, Erazim Kohák asks the question—"what though is the task of humans?" Beavers build dams and dragonflies glitter in the sun and microbes recycle the dead—"what though is the task of humans." And he answers, "we cherish its goodness and love its beauty and know its worth." To pause at the threshold of the beautiful is not mere refreshment but the act of worship.

*Sano Di Pietro*

Maximus the Great was one of medieval Europe's holiest men, and he paid a disciple's price in torture and exile. Yet surely he erred in one essential respect regarding God: "When in the full ardor of its love for God the mind goes out of itself, then it has no perception at all either of itself or of any creatures. For once illumined by the divine and infinite light, the mind remains insensible of anything that is made by him. . . . The one who has his mind tied to any earthly thing does not love God."[3]

On the contrary, we love God only when we fall in love with his creation. And when we are filled with the hunger to be creators also, and enlarge the universe with him.

I sometimes wonder, if God were to ask of me one question at life's end, which question would be the most penetrating, the most revealing, the most significant? I have in mind it would be some variation on the question, What beauty did you create?

The only really essential thing that changes in one's life is relationships. We can chart our life via job promotions and career reinventions, standards of living and places of residence. But when time and eternity blow all the dross away, will anything remain except the life history of our relationships? And are not relationships the supreme embodiment of the beautiful? The magnificent thing about love, which has made theologians wary of attributing love to God in the familiar sense of the term, is its sheer creative nature. When one enters into a relationship of loving reciprocity, one opens oneself to novelty. The interactions of two persons who become entwined in mutual caring and concern produce something never seen before: a communion, a relationship, a love whose dimensions cannot be predicted or constrained. That is as true of friends as it is of lovers. Love generates what scientists call emergent systems. One can dissect an ant to the subatomic level, but nothing in those gluons

*Giovanni di Benedetto & Workshop*

and quarks will tell you anything about how an ant colony will function. Such systems are more than the simple sum of their parts—they become infused with radical, unpredictable novelty. That is why love may be the most creative force of all.

We cannot all be Jane Austens or Van Goghs or architects or musicians. Yet we also contribute to the universe something magnificent and never seen before when we foster and nourish whatever communities are in our power to create. ✴

1.  Marilynne Robinson, *Gilead* (New York: Farrar, Straus and Giroux, 2004), 124.

2.  Nicholas Berdyaev, *The Divine and the Human,* trans. R. M. French (London: Geoffrey Bles, 1949), 139.

3.  Maximus the Confessor, *Four Hundred Chapters on Love.*

# WRITERS

**PAIGE CROSLAND ANDERSON** is an artist painting patterns while exploring notions about daily ritual, routine, and the creation of meaning through repeated acts.

**MADISON BAKER** makes art and comics about the little joyful things in life, domestic lives of nineteenth-century women, and The Church of Jesus Christ of Latter-day Saints.

**BISHOP ROBERT BARRON** is an American prelate of the Catholic Church who has served as bishop of the Diocese of Winona-Rochester since 2022 and is the founder of Word on Fire.

**SAMUEL BROWN** is a physician scientist who also wonders about bigger questions. He's parenting three children at the cusp of adulthood and writes books from time to time.

**GREG CHRISTENSEN** is a writer and creative director.

**D.A. COOPER** is a poet and writer from Houston, TX. He recently completed his MFA in poetry at the University of St. Thomas, Houston.

**GREER BATES CORDNER** is a PHD candidate in American religious history at Boston University School of Theology.

**JOHN ALBA CUTLER** is an associate professor of English at the University of California, Berkeley. He is a member of the Moraga Ward in the Oakland Stake.

**ZACHARY DAVIS** is the Executive Director of Faith Matters and the Editor of *Wayfare*.

**ELIZABETH C. GARCIA** is a Georgia native and mother of three. Her debut collection, *Resurrected Body*, received Cider Press Review's 2023 Editor's Prize.

**TERRYL GIVENS** is Senior Research Fellow at the Maxwell Institute and author and coauthor of many books, including *Wrestling the Angels* and *The God Who Weeps*.

**SHARLEE MULLINS GLENN** has published poetry, essays, short stories, and criticism in *Women's Studies*, *The Southern Literary Journal*, BYU *Studies*, *The New York Times*, and more. She is also an award-winning author of children's books.

**DEIDRE NICOLE GREEN** is an Assistant Professor of Latter-day Saint/Mormon Studies at Graduate Theological Union and publishes on constructive feminist theology, Kierkegaard, and Mormon Studies.

**MELISSA WEI-TSING INOUYE** (1979–2024) was a historian specializing in modern Chinese history, Christianity in China, women and religion, and the history of global Christianity.

**MIKAYLA JOHNSON** works as editor in chief at *Inscape* journal. Her work has been published or is forthcoming in *The Evermore Review*, AWE (*A Woman's Experience*), and *Dialogue*.

**TYLER JOHNSON** is a clinical associate professor of medicine and oncology at the Stanford University School of Medicine. He serves on the editorial boards of BYU *Studies* and *Wayfare* and has published widely on spirituality, ethics, medicine, culture, and modernity.

**LINDA HOFFMAN KIMBALL** is an author, artist, poet, and accidental activist. She has written, compiled, or illustrated sixteen books and has had her work included in many more. She has built and supported many community organizations, including Exponent II, Mormon Women for Ethical Government, and Segullah.

**MEGAN McMANAMA** is a voracious reader, podcast binger, and Zoom wrangler. She is also the cofounder of MomSense.

**WILLIAM MORRIS** writes and edits about Mormon literature. His most recent works are the novella *The Unseating of Dr. Smoot* and the collection *The Darkest Abyss: Strange Mormon Stories*.

**PETER MUGEMANCURO** is an undergraduate at Stanford University, studying economics.

**JON OGDEN** is a cofounder at UpliftKids.org, which helps families explore wisdom and timeless values together.

**ELIZABETH OLDFIELD** is the host of *The Sacred* and the author of *Fully Alive: Tending to the Soul in Turbulent Times*.

**STEVEN L. PECK** is an Associate Professor of Biology at Brigham Young University and the author of *A Short Stay in Hell* and *Heike's Void*.

**MARJORIE PERRY** is a multimedia freelance journalist with bylines in *The New York Times*, *The Economist*, *Slate*, and more.

**DUNCAN REYBURN** is an Associate Professor in the School of the Arts at the University of Pretoria. He is the author of *Seeing Things as They Are: G. K. Chesterton and the Drama of Meaning*.

**AMEI SHANK** is a medical student at Stanford University. She has lived in the United States, Singapore, and China, and hopes to continue growing the list.

**ROBERT SONNTAG** is an architect and artist seeking understanding through drawing and writing.

**SUNNY GRAMES STIMMLER** is an adjunct writing professor at American University, mother of two daughters, and a reluctantly aspiring polyglot thanks to twenty-five-plus years living overseas.

**ROBBIE TAGGART** is a teacher and poet who delights in the holiness of the everyday.

**CHARLES TAYLOR** is a professor emeritus of political science and philosophy at McGill University and the author of the acclaimed book *A Secular Age*.

**DAVID L. TAYMAN III,** a small business owner in North Georgia, blogs and tweets as "Improvement Era" on Latter-day Saint history, culture, scripture, and liturgy.

**MIKAYLA ORTON THATCHER** teaches anatomy and physiology at a local university and is the author of *Beehive Girl*.

**NATHAN THATCHER** is a composer, arranger, and author based in Saint Paul, Minnesota. He has collaborated with a wide array of musicians, working in concert music, pop music, film, television, and Broadway.

**EMILY UPDEGRAFF** lives in Wilmette, Illinois, where she works in university administration and is raising two teenagers. She is a bimonthly book review contributor at *Great Lakes Review* and has served as a features editor for *Exponent II*.

**FLEUR VAN WOERKOM** is a lover of earth, art, movement, and stories. She is currently studying writing at Columbia University.

**MATTHEW WICKMAN** is Professor of English at Brigham Young University. He teaches and writes on Christian spirituality, particularly the relationship between literature and spiritual experience. His most recent book is *Life to the Whole Being: The Spiritual Memoir of a Literature Professor*.

**CITLALLI H XOCHITIOTZIN ORTEGA** is a poet, philosopher, essayist, teacher, and cultural promoter at a national and international level.

**JANE ZWART** writes poetry, book reviews, interviews, and the occasional essay. Her work has appeared in *Poetry*, *TriQuarterly*, and *Threepenny Review*. She is a literature and writing professor at Calvin University, where she also codirects the Calvin Center for Faith & Writing.

# ARTISTS

# ARTISTS CONTINUED

*Caleb Williams*